Tina Houser's

EASTER-RIFIC!

teaching kids...
It's More than Just One Day!

©2011 Warner Press Inc Anderson, IN 46018
www.warnerpress.org
All rights reserved

ISBN: 978-1-59317-404-0

Editor: Karen Rhodes
Photography: Michael Meadows & Thinkstock.com
Design & Illustrations: Christian Elden & Kevin Spear

Printed in USA

31795017756

Warner
Press Kids
educate • nurture • inspire
www.warnerpress.org

Introduction

The week that transpires between the time of Jesus entering Jerusalem and His resurrection is jam-packed with significant stories. Jesus sure was busy in those few days! During that time He curses the fig tree, overturns the tables in the temple, is anointed by a passionate woman, has His last meal with His disciples, washes their feet, gives us the sacrament of communion, and prays in the Garden of Gethsemane. Peter denies that he knows Jesus and Judas betrays Him. And this is all before He goes to the cross!

Two Sundays. Yes, two Sundays! That's the amount of time we devote to teaching our kids about all of these incredible events. We cram it all in by devoting one sentence to each scene. But this week deserves more. It's the foundation of the Christian faith and we need to teach our children more diligently about each part of it.

Think about the possibilities if you celebrated and remembered Jesus' triumphal entry into Jerusalem—Palm Sunday—but did that in the middle of January. That would give you at least twelve weeks to really address what Jesus went through and what He felt was most important to do in His last days. Each meal, each parable, each moment shared with His disciples tells us something important about our Savior. Jesus didn't heal everyone who came to Him. He didn't attend every dinner or party that He was invited to. He didn't individually talk to all the people who wanted an audience with Him. What He did and what happened to Him in that last week was extremely significant. Each encounter was chosen for its impact, so that it would teach a divine lesson and further the Kingdom of God. Our children need to know the magnitude of each moment of Jesus' last week on Earth.

In the following pages you will find at least three activities, games, crafts, snacks, science experiments, storytelling ideas, and/or object lessons to help you teach nineteen of the stories that occurred during Holy Week. Then, you'll also find the same kind of elements for four more stories that happen before Jesus ascends to the Father. My prayer is that you will take these elements and use them to make each part of Jesus' last week come alive to your kids. The story of His death and resurrection is not ONE simple story!

I've had a deep conviction about teaching kids all of Easter for many years, and I'm tremendously thankful to have this opportunity to share some of my ideas for doing that. In these pages you'll also find two ways to do outreach during the Easter season and the particulars of those special events. Families who normally do not attend church throughout the year will include worship as part of their Easter celebration. So, a one-time special event may be just the way to connect with them during this time when their hearts are open.

So many children think Easter is about a new outfit, a Saturday egg hunt, and a basket of jellybeans and marshmallow chicks. Those things are fun, and I've used some of them in the activities that follow, but only as they can benefit the teaching of the Word. We can't allow the Truth to fall under the shadow of a giant rabbit costume. I believe there is a way to enjoy both the celebration of our culture and still keep our eyes fixed on Jesus. That's by making Holy Week more than two Sundays. Anticipate the resurrection for three months. Study it and celebrate everything that Jesus went through that week, so that when Easter Sunday arrives, your kids are ready to pull out all the stops and rejoice that...Jesus is alive!

Tina!

Table of Contents

Get a handle on this book . . .

When you go into a restaurant, you may not have eaten all day and you want appetizer, salad, soup, entrée with sides, and a big old dessert that should be eaten by at least four people. Or, you might be stopping in for a midnight snack and a cup of coffee. Sometimes you go with a couple of friends and other times you join a large party (which makes the waitress extremely nervous!). No matter what you're in the mood for or how many people you're sharing a meal with, the restaurant has something that will fit the bill.

Easter-rific is a menu. And I'm giving you permission to choose whatever fits your situation, your needs, and your desires. If you've locked yourself into the traditional two weeks of Easter celebration, then look into my eyes right now…I'm telling you it's okay to do more. It's okay to teach Easter for three weeks, six weeks, twelve weeks, or twenty weeks! Really!

How many and how much of the stories between Jesus entering Jerusalem and His ascension do you really want to address with your kids? It doesn't all have to be done in one year. But, I want you to think about giving kids the opportunity to let each story soak in. That can't happen in just two weeks. There's too much important stuff there!

So, what happens if you're the adventurous one and really do decide to go through every one of these stories beginning in mid-January? Some of the activities call for things like plastic eggs, Easter grass, marshmallow chicks, and chocolate eggs. Most stores don't pull out their Easter products quite that early (but the day after Valentine's Day it will appear). First of all, go ahead and pull out your own Easter decorations. You'll probably find some eggs and grass tucked away there. I know you probably already know this…because if you're in children's ministry, this is an understood fact of life…find something to substitute. Use real grass or shredded green tissue paper if the activity calls for Easter grass. And, there are always chocolate candies of some sort available, even if they don't look like decorated eggs. Don't lock yourself into having to have everything exactly as outlined. If you don't have a specific resource, then think of something that has similar properties and will serve the same purpose—something that you can get. We live in a wonderful age where, when all else fails, everything you need can be purchased year round on the Internet, if you plan ahead.

Notes

Jesus Enters Jerusalem (Palm Sunday)

Luke 19:28-39 (NIV)

Read the Scripture passage in whatever version you prefer. We have chosen NIV (New International Version), which we find more kid-friendly.

Bible Story

After Jesus had said this, he went on ahead, going up to Jerusalem. As he approached Bethphage and Bethany at the hill called the Mount of Olives, he sent two of his disciples, saying to them, "Go to the village ahead of you, and as you enter it, you will find a colt tied there, which no one has ever ridden. Untie it and bring it here. If anyone asks you, 'Why are you untying it?' say, 'The Lord needs it.'"

Those who were sent ahead went and found it just as he had told them. As they were untying the colt, its owners asked them, "Why are you untying the colt?"

They replied, "The Lord needs it."

They brought it to Jesus, threw their cloaks on the colt and put Jesus on it. As he went along, people spread their cloaks on the road.

When he came near the place where the road goes down the Mount of Olives, the whole crowd of disciples began joyfully to praise God in loud voices for all the miracles they had seen:

"Blessed is the king who comes in the name of the Lord!"

"Peace in heaven and glory in the highest!"

Some of the Pharisees in the crowd said to Jesus, "Teacher, rebuke your disciples!"

Key Element:

Jesus came into Jerusalem to celebrate the Passover with His disciples, knowing that this would be the last time He shared this special meal with them. People lined the streets and the celebration was wild as Jesus humbly rode a colt into the city. The children will not only learn this story, but will also share in the celebration of welcoming Jesus as King.

SNACK

Apple Slice Palms

Goodies:

- Large pretzel sticks
- Water
- Wedges of green apples

Gadgets:

- Green food coloring
- New craft paint brushes
- Paper plates
- Small dish

The Main Thing:

People laid their cloaks down in front of Jesus to show their respect. They also pulled leaves from the nearby trees to wave in the air and to lay before Him in celebration of His arrival in Jerusalem.

The Fun Stuff:

- Place on the paper plate a large pretzel which will be the trunk of the palm tree.
- The leaves of the palm tree will be made from wedges of apples.
- Tint a small dish of water with some green food coloring so the children can paint the raw apple with green-colored water.
- The children will position the wedges so they look like palm leaves coming out of the top of the pretzel trunk.

Carpet Roll Palm Trees

Resources Needed

- 2 artificial ferns
- 2 - 2" screws
- Burlap
- Empty carpet roll
- Hot glue
- Piece of wood, 2" x 4" x 36"
- Piece of plywood, 2-foot square

Resource Preparation:

- Think long-term resource when making these trees and you'll enjoy them in many different settings for years to come. Construct them in a variety of heights for a wonderful addition to your environment.

- Carpet rolls are a "throw-away" item at most carpet stores. Use a jigsaw to cut them the length that you want the trunk of your palm tree.

- Cut the burlap in strips that are about 6" wide and as long as your piece of material—the longer the better.

- Wrap the carpet roll with the burlap, using hot glue periodically to hold the burlap in place.

- Mount the piece of 2" x 4" wood onto the plywood so that it sticks up perpendicular in the center of the square.

- Use the two screws to screw through the plywood and into the 2" x 4" to hold it in place.

- The carpet roll will now slide down over the 2" x 4" post and the tree will stand.

- Insert the artificial ferns in the top of the carpet roll trunk and you've got a wonderful palm tree.

- The base can be covered with remnants of cloth or painted brown to be less conspicuous.

Clip-Clop, Clip-Clop

Resources Needed:

- 4 pairs of 4" cubes of wood
- Artificial tree
- Donkey clip art (see Appendix 6)
- Staple gun
- String
- Wide elastic

Resource Preparation:

- Beforehand, make 4 pairs of blocks that will fit onto the kids' feet. Each block will be a 4" x 4" piece of wood.

- Fasten a wide piece of elastic across one side of the wood, using a staple gun. This will be a stretchy strap to hold the feet in place. Use several staples in each end and make sure the elastic is long enough for a child to slip his foot between the block and the elastic without over-stretching the elastic.

- Make 9 copies of the donkey clip art.

- Write each of the questions listed below on a donkey and then tie a string to it.

- Tie each of these donkeys to an artificial tree or to something else in your room.

The Main Thing:

Read Zechariah 9:9. This was written hundreds of years before Jesus was even born. What does it sound like Zechariah is describing?

The Fun Stuff:

- Form two teams.
- The first player from each team will put a pair of the wooden donkey feet on.

- He will walk across the room, clip-clopping like a donkey, and then untie one of the questions.
- When he brings the question back to his team, clip-clop clip-clop, he will read it and give his answer.
- The next person should already have her donkey feet on and be ready to clip-clop to retrieve her question.

Questions:

- Who did Jesus send to get the donkey?
- What were the disciples supposed to say if someone asked them why they were taking the donkey?
- What did the disciples put on the back of the donkey for Jesus to sit on?
- What did the people put on the road in front of Jesus?
- What did the people wave in the air when Jesus came into Jerusalem?
- What was Jesus going to Jerusalem to celebrate?
- What did the people shout at Jesus as He passed by?
- When someone wanted the people to stop celebrating, what did Jesus say would celebrate and yell out?
- Why did the people want to see Jesus?

A Cloak Path

Resources Needed:

- Hand towels

The Fun Stuff:

- Play a game where each group will try to move one of their members from one side of the room to the other side.

- The children will work three at a time in this effort.

- One child will be Jesus who is trying to get to Jerusalem (the other side of the room).

- The other two children will each have a hand towel (cloak).

- They will lay their towel down in front of Jesus.

- As each towel is walked on, it will be picked up and placed in front of Jesus a little further in front of Him.

- The child playing Jesus will proceed across the room by walking on these towels as they are moved in front of Him.

Hands of Praise

Resources Needed:

- Accucut™ machine
- Green construction paper
- Green poster board
- Handprint die-cut or cut-out
- Lots of volunteers with scissors to help cut out handprints, if you don't have an Accucut™ machine
- Tape

Resource Preparation:

- **If you have access to an Accucut™** machine, this is a great all-church project. Even if your church doesn't have a die-cut machine, most schools have them, and the hand die-cut is a popular one. You may be able to borrow it. If you don't have access to a die-cut machine, trace someone's hand on white paper and make copies. Pass them out to people old enough to cut, along with a supply of green construction paper, and let them help you cut out enough for each person who attends worship for several weeks prior to Palm Sunday.

Hand them out or insert them in your worship bulletins, if you use bulletins.

The Fun Stuff:

- Encourage all congregants to write on the handprint what they would yell at Jesus if they were along the side of the road when He entered Jerusalem. (Make it simple…remember, it's something you would want Him to hear through the crowd.)
- Collect these.
- Tape each hand onto a piece of green poster board to make a gigantic palm leaf.
- Make sure the praises can be read on the hands.
- Cut around the edges of the posterboard, so the handprints make the edges of the leaf.
- Then, post these giant palms at the entryway so everyone can read the praises as they enter to worship on Palm Sunday.

Palm Leaf Stamping

Resources Needed:

- 9" x 12" pieces of construction paper
- Brown construction paper
- Glue
- Green craft paint
- Small paper plates
- Small pieces of material
- Soft kitchen sponges

The Fun Stuff:

- Cut a tree trunk from the brown paper and glue it to the 9" x 12" piece of paper.
- Cut the sponges into a simple palm leaf shape (an oval stretched out into points).
- Each child should have one sponge.
- Place a very thin layer of green paint on the paper plate.
- The children will dip their sponges into the paint and stamp leaves on the top of their trunks.
- They will need to reload their sponge every other time they stamp.
- Create a road for Jesus to travel on with scraps of material used for the cloaks that were laid before Him, and by sponge painting more leaves on craft paper.

Rolling through Jerusalem

Resources Needed:

- Cardboard boxes
- Croquet mallet
- Green construction paper
- Masking tape
- Paper towel rolls
- Sponge ball

Resource Preparation:

- Place a masking tape road about 10" wide on the floor.
- The older the children playing the more wiggles there can be in the road.
- Along the sides put some small cardboard boxes to represent the homes and shops of Jerusalem.
- If you want to get more elaborate, make some palm trees out of paper towel rollers and green construction paper to stand here and there.

The Main Thing:

Jesus sent two of his disciples into Jerusalem to get a young colt. When people in the town got word that Jesus was coming, they lined the roads and cheered for Him. They laid their cloaks and branches from the palm trees down on the road to cushion the path for the colt. Let's play a game about Jesus riding through the streets of Jerusalem.

Fun Stuff:

- Give the player a croquet mallet and a sponge ball.
- Pretend the ball is Jesus on the colt and He needs to go through Jerusalem.
- The child will tap the sponge ball (but cannot trap the ball) along the road, trying to keep it in between the masking tape lines.
- Take it slow! Jesus needs to greet the people along the way!

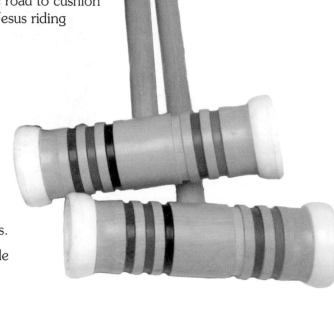

Curse on the Fig Tree

Matthew 21:18-22

Read the Scripture passage in whatever version you prefer. We have chosen NIV (New International Version), which we find more kid-friendly.

Bible Story

Early in the morning, as Jesus was on his way back to the city, he was hungry. Seeing a fig tree by the road, he went up to it but found nothing on it except leaves. Then he said to it, "May you never bear fruit again!" Immediately the tree withered.

When the disciples saw this, they were amazed. "How did the fig tree wither so quickly?" they asked.

Jesus replied, "Truly I tell you, if you have faith and do not doubt, not only can you do what was done to the fig tree, but also you can say to this mountain, 'Go, throw yourself into the sea,' and it will be done. If you believe, you will receive whatever you ask for in prayer."

Key Element:

The parable of the fig tree is not a parable that we often address, especially with children, and most definitely not during the celebration of Easter. But, it was during Jesus' last week here on earth that He lived this parable. He must have felt His time slipping away, so the things He chose to teach in those last days were important reminders of concepts He had already poured into His disciples. One more time Jesus wanted to tell His close circle of followers that God has created each person for a unique purpose, and if they aren't fulfilling that purpose and doing what is in God's plan, then they aren't living the life God envisioned for them. Through these activities, the children will be challenged to be all that God created them to be.

Balloon Fig Tree

Resources Needed:

- Clear packing tape
- Container
- Green balloons
- Paper clip
- Supply of multi-colored balloons
- Wide brown paper

Resource Preparation:

- From some wide brown paper (usually used as backgrounds for bulletin boards and can be purchased at a teacher supply store), cut out the trunk of a tree with some limbs going off in all directions.
- Tape this to the wall securely.
- Then, blow up green balloons and tape them to the limbs of the tree, using clear packing tape. These balloons will be the leaves of the fig tree.

The Main Thing:

When Jesus walked past the fig tree and saw that it had no fruit, He realized He had a wonderful opportunity to teach with this fig tree as His object lesson. Jesus was upset that the tree did not have figs on it, so He said out loud to the tree, but so the disciples could hear, that it would never again grow any fruit. What else is a fig tree good for besides producing figs? Nothing! The fig tree wasn't doing what it was created to do! Right then, the leaves withered and the tree dried up. Jesus used this fig tree as one of His parables. If He had told the disciples (and He probably did many times) that God expects them to show His love to others through their actions and words, in order that they might also believe, the disciples may or may not have remembered.

But, to teach them that lesson using this fig tree...well...I don't think they soon forgot His point! When we pass up opportunities to show God's love or open our mouths to speak God's truth, then we're like this fig tree that didn't produce fruit. We're not doing what God created us to do. Encourage the children to spend a few minutes thinking about opportunities when they could have done something or said something that God wanted them to, but didn't. These can be things that actually happened or things that the kids think of. (They will have an opportunity to share later in the activity.)

Fun Stuff:

- Beforehand, poke a hole in about half of the multi-colored balloons and then put the good balloons and the "holey" balloons in a container.

- In order for children to share an opportunity that was passed by, they must choose a balloon and blow into it.

- If they blow into the balloon and it blows up, then they take the balloon and sit down.

- If the balloon has a hole in it, then that balloon is not doing what it was created to do, just like the fig tree.

- They will share their missed opportunity. Then, give the child a paper clip that has been straightened out, to pop one of the leaf balloons on the tree.

- Continue doing this until all the leaves on the tree are withered (popped).

More Main Thing:

We don't want to be like the fig tree. God wants us to share His love with others. He wants us to tell others how He has made a difference in our lives. That's what He expects of each of us.

It's Bigger than I Thought

Resources Needed:

- 2 popcorn kernels
- Overhead projector
- Other small objects

Resource Preparation:

- For this activity, you're going to need an overhead projector. Go searching in a closet that hasn't been touched in a while and you'll probably find one collecting dust.
- Go ahead…what are you waiting for?

The Main Thing:

When the disciples witnessed Jesus causing the fig tree to dry up, Jesus told them if they had faith they could do big things also. Just a little faith can make a big difference. Our faith seems small, just like this little kernel of popcorn. But, God can do great things with our faith and make big things happen.

Fun Stuff:

- Show the kids the kernel of popcorn and say: "It sure seems small."
- Place the kernel on the overhead projector and then shine the image on the wall. Is it the same size now?
- Hold another kernel up against the wall where the image is being projected and compare the sizes.
- Let the kids find other small objects to place on the overhead projector to see how big they look on the wall.

More Main Thing:

What God wants most of all is to be with each of us. He wants us to stay in His presence and trust Him to lead our lives. He wants us to have faith in Him. Even when our faith is just beginning to grow, when it feels very small, God rewards that little bit of faith because He's so glad we are trusting Him.

Melting Styrofoam

Resources Needed:

- Glass bowl
- Pure Acetone (fingernail polish remover)
- Styrofoam™ peanuts

Resource Preparation:

- You will want to get fingernail polish remover that is pure acetone.

  (The kind that has water in it will work, but it will take a few minutes.)

The Main Thing:

When Jesus passed the fig tree that was supposed to be full of fruit and saw that it was bare—yes, completely empty—He said to it, "May you never bear fruit again." Immediately, the fig tree withered and died. Jesus made an object lesson out of this fruit tree. He wanted people to understand that if they aren't helping the kingdom and introducing others to God, then they are not producing fruit. That doesn't make God happy. People who are *not* introducing others to God are a fig tree without fruit!

Fun Stuff:

- Pour some pure acetone in the glass bowl.
- Then, place some Styrofoam™ peanuts in the bowl. Watch what happens.
- Just like the fig tree that withered, the peanuts get smaller and smaller. They wither and die.
- The kids will want to drop a peanut in, and this is fine as long as there is adult supervision with the fingernail polish remover (acetone).
- Keep putting the Styrofoam™ in the acetone.
- It's unbelievable how many peanuts will dissolve in the amount you've put in the bowl.

More Main Thing:

How does this experiment remind you of the fig tree story?

Jesus Clears the Temple

Mark 11:11-19

Read the Scripture passage in whatever version you prefer. We have chosen NIV (New International Version), which we find more kid-friendly.

Bible Story

Jesus entered Jerusalem and went into the temple courts. He looked around at everything, but since it was already late, he went out to Bethany with the Twelve.

The next day as they were leaving Bethany, Jesus was hungry. Seeing in the distance a fig tree in leaf, he went to find out if it had any fruit. When he reached it, he found nothing but leaves, because it was not the season for figs. Then he said to the tree, "May no one ever eat fruit from you again." And his disciples heard him say it.

On reaching Jerusalem, Jesus entered the temple courts and began driving out those who were buying and selling there. He overturned the tables of the money changers and the benches of those selling doves, and would not allow anyone to carry merchandise through the temple courts. And as he taught them, he said, "Is it not written: 'My house will be called a house of prayer for all nations'? But you have made it 'a den of robbers.'"

The chief priests and the teachers of the law heard this and began looking for a way to kill him, for they feared him, because the whole crowd was amazed at his teaching.

When evening came, Jesus and his disciples went out of the city.

Key Element:

God is holy. The place where He is worshiped is holy. Our lives go on—we buy and sell—but in the temple it was to be different. Every item and action in the temple was to point the people toward coming into God's presence. When the people set up a marketplace there, Jesus' blood began to boil. During these last days of His life, He couldn't stand the sight of His Father's house being treated in this manner. The children will learn that everything that takes place in the house of worship should honor our Heavenly Father.

OBJECT LESSON

Piggy bank

Resource Needed:

- Piggy bank with coins in it

Resource Preparation:

Use this object lesson to help children understand how the people who had to deal with the moneychangers and merchants at the temple may have felt.

- Hold up the piggy bank so the children can see.
- **Ask:**
  o What is this?
  o How many of you have something like this?
  o If yours isn't a pig, what does your bank look like?
  o Why do we put money in a piggy bank?
  o **Say:** Most of us use a piggy bank or some other kind of bank to put our money in while we're saving up for something special.

The Main Thing:

Can you remember something you saved up for and it took a while to get enough money in your piggy bank? You saved your pennies, nickels, dimes, quarters, and maybe even a dollar bill or two. They all went into the bank for that special day. Then, you finally had enough for the big purchase. You opened the piggy bank and took all the money out to count it. Then, you went to buy what you had been saving for. How did it feel to finally get what you had been saving for?
How would you have felt when you got to the store, if the clerk told you that the price had gone up? You don't have enough!

When the people who wanted to offer a sacrifice to God came to the temple, many times they were told that their animal wasn't good enough. Then, they had to buy a different animal that cost much more than it was worth. The people saved to give the best they had, and then they were told that it wasn't good enough...it wasn't the right kind to offer to God...it wasn't enough. Jesus saw what was going on in the temple and He was not happy. He was so upset with the moneychangers and the merchants that He turned their tables over, chased them out of the temple, and scattered their animals.

Rotten Eggs

Resources Needed:

- Masking tape

- Permanent marker

- Plastic eggs - enough for each child to have one.

Resource Preparation:

- Mark off a 10-foot square that will represent the temple.

- Draw some simple faces on the plastic eggs, so they can represent the moneychangers and the temple merchants.

- You'll need enough eggs for each child.

- Lay all the eggs in the center of the marked-off temple.

The Main Thing:

When Jesus went into the temple, He saw people selling animals for very high prices, to be used as sacrifices. He saw poor people being taken advantage of. He saw moneychangers cheating the people when they exchanged their money for the official temple coins. This was not the way it should be! The temple was supposed to be a place of prayer. Jesus couldn't tolerate their behaivor so He chased the moneychangers and merchants out of the temple. He flipped some of the tables over and coins went flying. The place of worship was not supposed to look like the market, and Jesus was going to clear the temple of any "rotten eggs."

The Fun Stuff:

- Choose three kids to start the play.

- Without touching any of the other eggs, the three players must choose one rotten egg in the temple and blow on it until it rolls outside the temple.

- There is no problem with them being inside the temple, but caution the kids that as they move to blow on their egg, they cannot kick or move any other egg.

- When their rotten egg rolls out of the temple, they will pick up the egg and go tag someone else to do the same.

- The game is over when the temple is cleared of all the rotten eggs!

Sneaky Temple Merchants

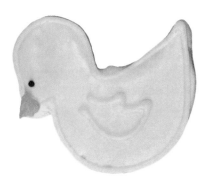

Resources Needed:

- 25 Styrofoam™ cups
- Dark cloth
- Marshmallow chicks
- Small ball

Resource Preparation:

- On the table place all 25 Styrofoam™ cups upside down.
- Under one of the cups put a marshmallow chick.
- Once you get your grass place settings set up, experiment to see where you should designate the stand-behind line. (See Appendix 7, page 140 for the place-setting pattern.)

The Fun Stuff:

- Choose a child to come to the cups (first player).
- Tell that child that the marshmallow chick under one of the cups belongs to him, but he can't have it right now.
- Choose another child to be the temple merchant.
- The temple merchant will stand at the table with the cups, and then roll the ball to the other end of the room.
- When he rolls it, the child standing with him at the cups will have to chase it.
- While the child is chasing the ball to bring it back to the table, the temple merchant will look under the cups to see if he can find the marshmallow chick.
- The cup must be returned to its upside down position each time the temple merchant looks under one.
- If the merchant finds the chick, he gets to keep it.
- If the player makes it back with the ball before the merchant can find the chick, then he gets to keep his marshmallow chick. (At this point, the child will simply look under the cups until the chick is found.)
- Now, hold a dark cloth up in front of the table while you place another marshmallow chick under a cup. This way the kids won't be tempted to peak when they should have their eyes closed.
- Choose two more players and continue playing in this manner as long as you like.

The Main Thing:

When people brought their sacrifices to the temple, they were inspected, because a sacrifice was supposed to be a perfect animal. If there was a blemish on the animal, the person would have to purchase a new animal in order to make a sacrifice. The temple merchants took advantage of people, especially poor people, and charged them high prices for the sacrificial animals. They cheated the people. It's almost like when the person wasn't looking, the merchant stole from him.

In our game today, the temple merchant tried to take advantage of the player while he was chasing the ball, so the merchant could take the marshmallow chick for himself. Jesus was really upset by this, because the temple was a place of prayer, not a place to run a questionable business…or any business at all.

Parable of the Marriage Feast

Matthew 22:1-14

Read the Scripture passage in whatever version you prefer. We have chosen NIV (New International Version), which we find more kid-friendly.

Bible Story

Jesus spoke to them again in parables, saying: "The kingdom of heaven is like a king who prepared a wedding banquet for his son. He sent his servants to those who had been invited to the banquet to tell them to come, but they refused to come.

"Then he sent some more servants and said, 'Tell those who have been invited that I have prepared my dinner: My oxen and fattened cattle have been butchered, and everything is ready. Come to the wedding banquet.'

"But they paid no attention and went off—one to his field, another to his business. The rest seized his servants, mistreated them and killed them. The king was enraged. He sent his army and destroyed those murderers and burned their city.

"Then he said to his servants, 'The wedding banquet is ready, but those I invited did not deserve to come. So go to the street corners and invite to the banquet anyone you find.' So the servants went out into the streets and gathered all the people they could find, the bad as well as the good, and the wedding hall was filled with guests.

"But when the king came in to see the guests, he noticed a man there who was not wearing wedding clothes. He asked, 'How did you get in here without wedding clothes, friend?' The man was speechless.

"Then the king told the attendants, 'Tie him hand and foot, and throw him outside, into the darkness, where there will be weeping and gnashing of teeth.'

"For many are invited, but few are chosen."

Key Element:

Here's another parable—one of those wonderful little stories that Jesus told at the last minute. The Jews, who God had cared for and loved as His people for so long, had rejected Him just like the invited wedding guests rejected their invitation to the feast. Jesus threw open His arms and pointed out that God will welcome all those that the Jews have despised. Your children will learn that God does not label, categorize or eliminate based on the judgments of this world. There will be a great celebration at the Lord's table some day and we are all invited. The harsh truth is that some will accept that invitation and others won't.

Imposter Tag

Resources Needed:

- 3 bandanas

Resource Preparation:

- You'll need a large open area that will be good for a rowdy game of tag.
- Give three kids the colored bandanas to poke into the top of their pants, so they have a tail.
- These kids will represent the man who came to the wedding dressed in rags.
- No one would go to a wedding dressed in rags, especially when they had been given beautiful wedding clothes to wear!
- The king threw the man out, so we're going to throw these three out also.

The Fun Stuff:

- Choose two kids to be "It."
- They will try to tag the three with the bandanas—rags.
- All the other kids who don't have bandanas will run around because as soon as one of the "Its" has pulled a bandana out, the bandana will be thrown on the ground.
- Anyone who picks up the bandana can be free for five seconds while they make their bandana tail, and become the man who wore rags to the wedding. (I suggest they keep running while they are doing this or they'll be caught real quickly.)

26

Ping Pong Guests

Resources Needed:

- Easter grass
- Permanent markers
- Ping pong balls

Resource Preparation:

- Give each child a ping pong ball.
- He or she will draw on the ball with the permanent markers so that the ball resembles him or her.
- On the floor, place little piles of the Easter grass as if they are place settings at a table. (You can even lay a table there or mark a pretend one with masking tape.)

The Main Thing:

Jesus told a parable about a king who gave a big feast for his son's wedding.

Lots of people were invited, but when the time came for everyone to sit down for the feast, no one had shown up. The king sent his messengers out to get his guests, but they still didn't come. So, the king told his servants that the people who were invited didn't deserve his feast. The king had the city burned where the invited guests lived.

Then, the king sent his servants out in every direction with the instructions to invite everyone. It didn't matter if they were rich or poor, young or old. Each person was given a special wedding robe to wear to the feast. When they all sat down for the feast, the king noticed that one man wasn't wearing the special robe that the king had given him. The man had no reason for not wearing the robe, so the king had him thrown out. Jesus told this parable to help people understand that the Jews had been God's special people and had been invited to join Him, but they had refused, just like the invited guests.

God was now inviting all people to be His special people, no matter who they were, but they were expected to honor Him. The man who did not wear the robe did not honor the king. God wants all of us to be with Him. He wants all of us to repent and become His special people. He wants all of us to honor Him. Like in the parable, God wants us to join Him at His table for the celebration feast.

The Fun Stuff:

- The kids will bounce their ping pong balls on the ground and try to get them to come to rest in one of the grass place settings.
- When their ball is seated at the table, they should yell, "I'm at the Lord's feast!"

You've Got a Waffle Face

Resources Needed:

- Cleaned and sliced fruit
- Paper plates
- Round frozen waffles
- Squirt whipped cream

The Fun Stuff:

- Each child will get a small round waffle that has been warmed.
- Provide them with sliced fruit (like bananas, tangerines, kiwi) and other fruit that is whole (like different kinds of berries and grapes).
- The kids will create a face on their waffle using a squirt whipped topping as the glue to hold the fruit in place.
- The only part of the face that they should not attach is the mouth.
- The mouth should be moveable.

The Main Thing:

How did the king feel when his original guests had excuses for not coming to the wedding feast for his son and bride? Move the fruit that makes up your mouth to express how the king felt. This is the way God feels when we don't accept His invitation to believe in His Son Jesus and join Him at the table.

How did the king feel when his new guests arrived? Move the mouth fruit to express how the king felt. God celebrates when all of us, no matter what nationality, no matter if we are male or female, no matter if we are 10 years old or 97 years old, no matter if we live in the city or live in a cabin in Alaska…join the heavenly feast!

How did the king feel when the one guest came in rags rather than the wedding clothes the king had provided for him? Move the fruit to express how the king felt. God has given us what we need to be able to be part of His heaven. He's given us Jesus. There's no way to join God at His heavenly feast without accepting Jesus—putting on the robe of forgiveness that only comes through Him.

Paying Taxes

Mark 12:13-17

Read the Scripture passage in whatever version you prefer. We have chosen NIV (New International Version), which we find more kid-friendly.

Bible Story

Later they sent some of the Pharisees and Herodians to Jesus to catch him in his words. They came to him and said, "Teacher, we know that you are a man of integrity. You aren't swayed by others, because you pay no attention to who they are; but you teach the way of God in accordance with the truth. Is it right to pay the imperial tax to Caesar or not? Should we pay or shouldn't we?"

But Jesus knew their hypocrisy. "Why are you trying to trap me?" he asked. "Bring me a denarius and let me look at it." They brought the coin, and he asked them, "Whose image is this? And whose inscription?"

"Caesar's," they replied.

Then Jesus said to them, "Give back to Caesar what is Caesar's and to God what is God's.

And they were amazed at him.

Key Elements:

Taxes are of this world and they won't exist in heaven (thank goodness!). Go ahead and take care of the things that make this world function politically and economically. But, the bigger picture is that we need to give God what He deserves...each life that He created—in humble obedience to Him. The children will learn that they need to take care of the things that make life happen, but their greater life purpose is in giving themselves to His will.

Give to Josie What Is Josie's

Resources Needed:

- Basket
- Goodies for inside eggs
- Mid-size spoons
- Permanent marker
- Plastic eggs
- Slips of paper

Resource Preparation:

- Write the name of each child on one of the filled plastic eggs. Then, send all those eggs outside with some helpers who will hide them.
- Meanwhile, the kids will write their names on a slip of paper, fold it twice and then put it in the basket.
- After all the kids have put their names in the basket, each child will draw out a new slip.
- The name on this slip will tell them which egg they will be searching for.
- While they are waiting for eggs to be hidden, instruct them on how the hunt will be conducted.
- Each child will get a spoon—the middle-size spoon in your flatware.
- When the leader gives the signal, the children will take their spoons and go looking for the egg that has their person's name on it.
- When they find it, they can only touch it with the spoon. No hands.
- The egg must then be carried to the person whose name is on it.
- The only problem is that everybody's moving around! The person receiving the egg can take it with his or her hand once the egg is within reach.
- Also, warn the kids not to say aloud the names they see on eggs that are not their person's egg.
- Everyone has to find his or her egg without help from someone else.

The Main Thing:

When Jesus was asked about whether or not the Jewish people should pay the tax to Caesar, Jesus answered, "Give to Caesar what is Caesar's. Give to God what is God's." We've taken our eggs today and given them to the people they belong to. We didn't give them to someone else. Jesus was fine with the people giving Caesar the coins that had Caesar's picture on them. But, He wanted them to know that what belonged to God was much more than a coin…it was their lives…and they needed to give their lives to God.

The Fun Stuff:

- Now open your eggs and see what's inside just for you.

Jelly Bean on a Stick

Resources Needed:

- Bowl
- Chopsticks
- Clear packing tape
- Containers
- Jellybeans

Resource Preparation:

- Tape one jellybean of each color on the outside of a container, so that you have one container marked for yellow, one for red, one for green, and so on.
- The kids will use a pair of chopsticks to pick up a jellybean out of the bowl and carry it to the container with the matching color.
- The colors belong together.
- Rather than use the chopsticks the traditional way, the kids can hold one in each hand and balance a jellybean atop the chopsticks.

The Main Thing:

The Jews did not like to pay taxes to the Roman emperor, Caesar. They also didn't like the things that Jesus was saying. So, they asked Jesus a question because they thought they could trick Him. They asked if it was right or wrong to pay taxes to Caesar.

Jesus asked them for a coin. When He looked at it, there was a picture of Caesar stamped on both sides. Jesus told them to give to Caesar what was Caesar's, like the coin. But, Jesus also said to give God what belongs to Him…and that would be our whole selves.

Jesus matched the coin with Caesar because they were alike. He matched our lives to God because we are supposed to be like Him. The coin belonged to Caesar and we belong to God.

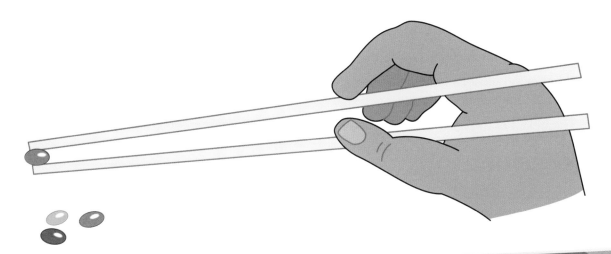

 **Pay Your Taxes**

Resources Needed:

- Bucket
- Coins (fake or real)
- Extra large men's T-shirt
- Masking tape
- Paper lunch sack

Resource Preparation:

- This is a hilarious game. The kids will play in pairs, and you can have as many pairs going at the same time as you like.
- Place some coins in a paper sack for each pair; then, put the sacks on a table at one side of the room.
- At the far end of the room, place a bucket with a stand-behind masking tape line marked about 10-feet away from the bucket.

The Fun Stuff:

- Each pair of kids will get inside an extra large men's T-shirt together so that each person will have one arm coming through a sleeve and one arm inside the T-shirt.
- At the signal, the pair will run to get their paper sack.
- They will then take their sack to the stand-behind line by the bucket.
- One person must be holding the bag at all times, but they can switch back and forth. They just can't set the bag down.
- The object of the game is for each pair to pay their taxes and toss five coins into the bucket.

The Main Thing:

Give to Caesar what is Caesar's! So, here's the tax, Caesar. We may give money to the government for tax, but what is it that we give to God? After all, God is much greater than any government. What does God deserve from us? What should we willingly give Him?

Most Important Commandment

Matthew 22:34-40

Read the Scripture passage in whatever version you prefer. We have chosen NIV (New International Version), which we find more kid-friendly.

Bible Story

Hearing that Jesus had silenced the Sadducees, the Pharisees got together. One of them, an expert in the law, tested him with this question: "Teacher, which is the greatest commandment in the Law?"

Jesus replied: "'Love the Lord your God with all your heart and with all your soul and with all your mind.' This is the first and greatest commandment. And the second is like it: 'Love your neighbor as yourself.' All the Law and the Prophets hang on these two commandments."

Key Elements:

Jesus was about to give everything in service to His Heavenly Father. He leaves us with a commandment that parallels His actions—to love the Lord your God with all your heart, soul and mind. It's almost as if Jesus is saying, "Watch me. Do as I am about to do, and do it out of obedience to the Father's will. Give everything you have to give." The children will be challenged to give themselves totally over to God and to love Him passionately.

Giving It All—Heart, Soul and Mind

Resources Needed:

- Baking soda
- Clear vase
- Glass baking pan
- Juice glass
- Vinegar
- Water

Resource Preparation:

- Beforehand, prepare a clear vase with 2 parts water and 1 part vinegar.

    (The easiest way to do this is with a juice glass. Fill the glass twice with water and pour it in the vase; then fill the glass once with vinegar and pour it in.)

- You want the water level to be less than ½" from the top, so keep filling 2:1 until it reaches the top. Place this vase in the glass baking pan, which will act as a spill basin.

The Main Thing:

When Jesus said to love the Lord God with all your heart, soul, and mind, is there anything left? No, that's everything. That's every part of us. That's what He was saying—we are to love God with everything we can possibly love Him with.

The Fun Stuff:

- **Say:** This vase represents us, and the liquid in it is everything that is in us—our heart, soul and mind. Let's give all of our mind, all our thoughts, all our figuring, to God.
- Drop a spoonful of baking soda down in the vase.
- Immediately, it will bubble over with foam.
- Point out that there is still more of you in there.
- "Let's give God all of your soul."
- Drop another spoonful of baking soda down in the vase.
- More bubbling, but there's still more left.
- Drop more baking soda in to represent giving God all of your heart.

More Main Thing:

When the foam goes down there will probably be some liquid still in the bottom of the vase. Pick up the vase and say, "God wants us to be poured out for Him, giving Him our all." One of the important things that Jesus wanted to teach about that last week of His life was to love the Lord God with all your heart, soul, and mind.

OBJECT LESSON # Love Air

Resource Needed:

- Balloons

The Fun Part:

- Hold up a balloon that has no air in it.

- Try to bat it around like you would a balloon that has air in it.

- Complain about it not being fun this way!

- What would change this balloon?

- How can we make this balloon be something really fun and special?

- Pass out the balloons.

- Each child should choose a person in his/her life—it doesn't need to be someone they know really well. Thinking only of that person, share a way that you can show love to him or her.

- When they share a way, then they should put a big puff of air in the balloon. Continue thinking of ways you can show love to this person and keep adding air to your balloon. Say: You've put a lot of love in these balloons! Tie them off now so you can keep all that love air inside.

- How are the balloons different than when we started?

- How do you think the person you were thinking about could be different because of the way you show them love?

- Do you think your love can change that person?

- How does showing love change other people?

The Main Thing:

Jesus declared what the most important thing for us to do is. He said the most important thing is to love the Lord God with all your heart, and with all your soul, and with all of your mind (Matthew 22:37). But then, He went on to say that there's another very, very important commandment right behind that one. That second most important commandment is to love other people as much as you love yourself (Matthew 22:39). Can you think of someone who is difficult for you to love? If you had another empty balloon, could you think of enough ways to show love to them that would fill that balloon?

Post the Rules

Resources Needed:

- 8 pieces of light-colored construction paper
- Pens or pencils
- Post-It™ notes

Resource Preparation:

- Make 8 signs from the construction paper.
- Write one of the following on each sign:
  - At Grandma's house
  - On the beach
  - In a fancy restaurant
  - At church
  - In a doctor's office
  - In your school classroom
  - On the playground
  - In the kitchen

Put the signs up all over the room with plenty of space between them. Give each child eight Post-It™ notes and something to write with.

The Main Thing:

Talk about what Jesus said is the most important commandment. He said it is most important to "Love the Lord your God with all your heart, and with all your soul, and with all your mind." He also added that the second most important commandment is to "Love your neighbor as yourself." All the other rules come under one of these two most important commandments. If you're tempted to lie about a friend, you know that's wrong because that's not loving your neighbor. If you're tempted to skip out on church, that's not honoring God. If you're tempted not to help someone who needs help, then you aren't loving your neighbor.

Can you name some more situations like this and tell which of the two most important commandments they fall under?

The Fun Stuff:

- Have kids write down the most important rules that come under these commandments and then stick the Post-It™ close to the sign it goes with.

A Widow's Offering

Mark 12:41-44

Read the Scripture passage in whatever version you prefer. We have chosen NIV (New International Version), which we find more kid-friendly.

Bible Story

Jesus sat down opposite the place where the offerings were put and watched the crowd putting their money into the temple treasury. Many rich people threw in large amounts. But a poor widow came and put in two very small copper coins, worth only a few cents.

Calling his disciples to him, Jesus said, "Truly I tell you, this poor widow has put more into the treasury than all the others. They all gave out of their wealth; but she, out of her poverty, put in everything—all she had to live on."

Key Elements:

Jesus points out that the widow gave everything she had, and He does this just a few days before He demonstrates giving everything Himself. Is it a humble gift we learn about? A generous gift? An obedient gift? Or a gift that came from an overwhelming gratitude? It's all there, and the children will find their own personal connection to the widow and her gift as they learn about this story.

Give It Up

Resources Needed:

- Malted milk ball Easter egg candies
- Metal bowl
- Small paper cups

Resource Preparation:

- Beforehand, put 10-15 malt ball candies in small paper cups for the kids. You don't want these to be equal amounts, but similar.
- In one of the cups, though, put only 2 malt ball candies.
- Give each child a cup and make it very obvious that there are different amounts in each cup.

The Main Thing:

In Mark 12:41-44, the Bible tells us about a time when Jesus was sitting in the temple, watching the people put their gifts in the offering box. He noticed that the rich people were giving a lot of money, but they still had lots left at home. Then, He saw a poor widow woman pull out two coins and put them in the offering. Jesus told the disciples who were with Him that this widow woman gave more than the rich people. The rich people gave out of what they didn't need; it was extra money to them. But the widow woman gave everything she had, and there was no extra money at home.

Jesus wants us to give extravagantly and He wants us to give our whole selves. He was pleased with this woman who was so grateful for God being in her life that she wanted to give everything.

Some people call themselves Christians, but they only go to church when they don't have a game to go to, or an overnighter, or a family party.

And some people only sing praises when they can be up in front of a crowd and people are watching them. They only give to God when it's convenient or they get some attention.

That's *not* how the widow woman gave. It was very inconvenient for her to give her last two coins and she surely didn't do anything that would make people pay attention to her. Jesus is happy when we give all of ourselves to Him.

The Fun Stuff:

- **Say:** Let's pretend these malted milk balls represent everything you have to eat today. We know that we should give them all to God.
- All of you please put two of your malted milk ball candies in the metal bowl in the center of the table. (Some of the kids will do what you say without question. Others may try to sneak and only put one in.)

- Does anyone want to give away some extra malted milk balls and put them in the bowl?

- Now, everyone count the number of candies you have left in your cup.

- Identify the child who had only two malted milk balls to begin with and ask him or her how many he or she has left.

- **Ask:** If that was everything you had to eat today, what are you going to eat now that you've given away both the candies that you had to begin with?

Ask the whole class:

- Was it more difficult to put two candies in the bowl for the person who had two candies to begin with or the person who had 12?

Give Your Treasure

Resources Needed:

- A large wooden cross
- Art paper
- Markers
- Tacks

Activity:

- Instruct the children to draw a picture of themselves with the thing they treasure most in their life.

- **Say:** Draw it big so everyone can tell what it is. If it's a game you like to play, then draw you and your friends playing it. If it's your cell phone, then draw a picture of you talking on your cell phone.

The Main Thing:

In Mark 12:41-44 we hear about a widow woman who put her last two coins in the offering box. Jesus said that she gave more than the rich people who gave a bunch of money. He was pleased with her, because she gave all that she had. Nothing was so important that it couldn't be given to God.

Activity:

- Prop the wooden cross against the wall.

- **Say:** Jesus gave up His most treasured possession and that was His life. He gave up heaven and came to earth. He did that to give up His life as a payment for our sins.

- **Ask:** Is there any way that we could ever give Him as much as He has given us?

- **Say:** What Jesus gave us is bigger than the two coins the woman put in the offering box. When you look at your picture of the thing you treasure most, I can tell you that what Jesus gave for you is even bigger than your treasure.

- Ask the children to come one at a time and attach their picture to the cross.

- If any of the children feel they could actually do it, ask them to say: I love Jesus so much that I would give up my [treasure] for Him.

Closing Prayer:

Dear Heavenly Father, help us to always be willing givers and to always make You our most precious treasure. Thank You for giving the gift of Your big love to us. Amen.

Two Pennies in a Basket

Resources Needed:

- 5 Easter baskets
- Pennies

Resource Preparation:

- Set up five Easter baskets at the far end of the room.
- Choose five kids to play at a time. (You can change the number of kids playing by increasing or decreasing the number of baskets to suit your size group and room situation.)

The Fun Stuff:

- Each player will place two pennies on his or her forehead.
- At the signal all the players will try to move to their basket without dropping their pennies. If a penny falls off, the player must return to the starting line and begin again.
- The first player to get his or her two pennies into his or her basket gets 100 points and the chance to earn another 100 points by answering a question about the story of the widow's offering.
- After the winner of each round answers his or her question, choose five new kids to participate for the next question.

Questions for Fun Stuff:

- How much did the rich people put into the treasury box?
- How much did the widow put into the treasury box?
- Why do you think Jesus noticed the widow?
- How did Jesus know who was rich?
- What did Jesus say about the gift of the rich people?
- What did Jesus say about the gift of the widow?
- Why did the widow's gift impress Jesus more than the rich man's gift?
- Why do you think Jesus wanted to talk to His disciples about what they saw at the temple?

Woman with Perfume

Mark 14:3-9

Read the Scripture passage in whatever version you prefer. We have chosen NIV (New International Version), which we find more kid-friendly.

Bible Story

Jesus was in Bethany. He was at the table in the home of a man named Simon, who had a skin disease. A woman came with a special sealed jar of very expensive perfume. It was made out of pure nard. She broke the jar open and poured the perfume on Jesus' head.

Some of the people there became angry. They said to one another, "Why waste this perfume? It could have been sold for more than a year's pay. The money could have been given to poor people." So they found fault with the woman.

"Leave her alone," Jesus said. "Why are you bothering her? She has done a beautiful thing to me. You will always have poor people with you. You can help them any time you want to. But you will not always have me. She did what she could. She poured perfume on my body to prepare me to be buried. What I'm about to tell you is true. What she has done will be told anywhere the good news is preached all over the world. It will be told in memory of her."

Key Element:

Anointing signified being chosen for a special service to God. Without knowing the full meaning of what the following days would hold, this woman anointed Jesus, because she knew He had been chosen by God for a special mission. The children will learn that their attitude should be that of Christ, ready and willing to serve the mission they are called to.

Giant Egg Piñata

Resources Needed:

- Craft paints
- Dowel rod
- Large balloon
- Newspaper
- Paint brushes
- Plastic table covering
- String
- Water
- White glue
- White paper

The Main Thing:

When the woman opened the bottle and poured the perfume on Jesus, she spilled out everything that was inside her container. She emptied both the bottle and herself in front of Jesus. We're going to make a piñata to celebrate Easter. When it is broken, everything in it will be spilled out and our piñata will be emptied.

Resource Preparation:

- Make an egg piñata any size you like by choosing the size of balloon you will use.
- Blow the balloon up to the size you'd like your piñata and tie it off.
- Place a dowel rod between two chairs. Tie a piece of string to the neck of the balloon and to the dowel rod, so the balloon will hang while you work on it.
- Cut the newspaper into strips about 1" wide and about 8" long.
- Make a mixture of half water and half white glue. You may have to stir the mixture occasionally as you work. You'll also want to put this in a bowl that is easy to clean or is disposable.
- Run the newspaper strips through the glue mixture and remove the extra by running the strip lightly between your fingers.
- Smooth the strip of newspaper onto the balloon, wiping out any major bumps or wrinkles.
- Keep applying the strips of paper until the balloon is completely covered. Leave a little bit of balloon showing where the string is tied to the knot.
- Let the piñata dry overnight.

- The next day add another similar layer, letting it dry overnight again. Four layers is the maximum to apply; but three is usually sufficient. Make sure each layer is completely dry before adding the next layer. On the last layer, use white paper instead of newspaper. That will make it easier to paint.

- Once the last layer is dry, pop the balloon and pull it out of the piñata. The piñata is now ready to paint like it is a giant Easter egg.

- Fill it with small candies through the hole at the top.

- To hang the piñata, poke four holes around the larger hole at the top. Thread a piece of yarn through each hole and then bring the pieces of yarn together and tie them in a knot. You can attach a longer string to the yarn so that the piñata can hang from a tree limb or wherever. Reinforce the piñata where the yarn goes through the holes by applying some packing tape or masking tape around the holes. When treated roughly (and a piñata always is), the yarn may pull through the papier-mâché.

- Alternate papier-mâché paste: Use liquid starch that can be purchased in the detergent aisle at the local grocery store.

Homemade Perfume

Resources Needed:

- 2 cups of fresh chopped flower blossoms
- 4 cups of water
- Bowl
- Cheesecloth
- Old saucepan

Resource Preparation:

- In the bowl, place a piece of cheesecloth so the edges are hanging over the sides of the bowl.
- Put two cups of flower blossoms in the bowl. Any flowers will do, but ones with a potent fragrance (like lavender, lilac, rose and honeysuckle) will work best.
- Now, pour water over the petals until they are completely covered. Let this set overnight.
- The next day, pull the edges of the cheesecloth up and around the blossoms to make a bundle. Gently squeeze the cheesecloth so that any water still in the bundle will drip out into the bowl.
- Put the water that is in the bowl (the flower "juice") into the old saucepan. Simmer this until there are just a couple of tablespoons left in the saucepan.
- That is your perfume.

The Main Thing:

The woman who poured the perfume on Jesus may have made it herself, or it may have been a gift to her from someone special, or maybe she had saved her money to purchase the perfume for herself. We don't really know how she came to have it, but we do know that it was considered worth quite a bit of money and that she willingly gave all of it to Jesus.

Lots of Pieces

Resources Needed:

- Bottle with a wide mouth
- Spray perfume
- Tissue paper

Resource Preparation:

- Spread the sheets of tissue paper out flat. Lightly spray them with the perfume.
- Tear the tissue paper into very small pieces and put them in a bottle that has a wide mouth. A cappuccino bottle usually has a nice size opening.
- The tissue papers need to be small enough that the pieces will easily pour out of the bottle. Now you have a prop that is especially appropriate for preschoolers.
- The use of the bottle and the scented tissue paper utilizes two of their senses.

The Main Thing:

Read the scripture, Mark 14:3-9, or tell this story in your own words. When you get to the part where the woman pours out the perfume on Jesus' head, turn your bottle upside down and pour out the tissue paper pieces in front of you. Leave them there while you continue with the story.

The people watching did not understand why Jesus wasn't upset with the woman. His response to that was to tell everyone that she was preparing Him for His burial. Jesus came to live among us here on Earth in order to beat death by going to the cross and leaving death to live again. When we accept that, He will take the pieces of our lives that seem messed up, and help us pull them back together.

Scrape up the pieces of tissue paper into a pile.

Say: *All the possessions the woman had were represented in that expensive perfume, and she gave it all.*

Foot Washing

John 13:1-17

Read the Scripture passage in whatever version you prefer. We have chosen NIV (New International Version), which we find more kid-friendly.

Bible Story

It was just before the Passover Festival. Jesus knew that the hour had come for him to leave this world and go to the Father. Having loved his own who were in the world, he loved them to the end.

The evening meal was in progress, and the devil had already prompted Judas, the son of Simon Iscariot, to betray Jesus. Jesus knew that the Father had put all things under his power, and that he had come from God and was returning to God; so he got up from the meal, took off his outer clothing, and wrapped a towel around his waist. After that, he poured water into a basin and began to wash his disciples' feet, drying them with the towel that was wrapped around him.

He came to Simon Peter, who said to him, "Lord, are you going to wash my feet?"

Jesus replied, "You do not realize now what I am doing, but later you will understand."

"No," said Peter, "you shall never wash my feet."

Jesus answered, "Unless I wash you, you have no part with me."

"Then, Lord," Simon Peter replied, "not just my feet but my hands and my head as well!"

Jesus answered, "Those who have had a bath need only to wash their feet; their whole body is clean. And you are clean, though not *every* one of you." For he knew who was going to betray him, and that was why he said not *every* one was clean.

When he had finished washing their feet, he put on his clothes and returned to his place. "Do you understand what I have done for you?" he asked them. "You call me 'Teacher' and 'Lord,' and rightly so, for that is what I am. Now that I, your Lord and Teacher, have washed your feet, you also should wash one another's feet. I have set you an example that you should do as I have done for you. Very truly I tell you, no servant is greater than his master, nor is a messenger greater than the one who sent him. Now that you know these things, you will be blessed if you do them.

Key Element:

Jesus modeled a lifestyle, just a few hours before His arrest. Can't you just sense Jesus' heart that's pleading, "Don't just talk about it, guys. Live it. Show people how much you love them and how much God loves them by the way you serve them. Be willing to do the dirty work."

The children may never have seen the act of foot washing. The act of washing one another's feet is a beautiful thing to be part of, but so much more important is the way we live our lives day in and day out in that same mindset. Children are so willing to serve, but they must intentionally be taught so that it also becomes their lifestyle.

Let Me Show You

Resource Needed:

- A shoe that ties

The Fun Stuff:

Tell the kids you are going to teach them how to do something. Then, read these instructions straight through at a fairly quick pace.

- Take the right lace and cross it over the left lace, grasping the laces together where they have formed an X. The right lace will go down, under and through the left lace.

- Grab the right lace in your left hand and the left lace in your right and pull them tightly. You have formed the first knot.

- Form a loop holding it with your right index finger and thumb close to the shoe.

- Take the left lace and go around the loop. Feel for the thumb on your right hand and that's where you will push the lace through. Grasp the emerging loop with your right thumb and index finger.

- Slip your left hand to the top of the left loop. Pull on both loops until they are tight.

- Check by feeling the length of your loops to make them even. Check the length of the ties to make sure they aren't too long.

What was I teaching you to do? (Tie your shoes) *If you didn't know how to tie your shoes and you heard me read this off, would you know how to do it then? Does that ever happen to you? Someone tells you how to do something. You listen, but it just doesn't seem to soak in? What would help you understand how to tie your shoes? If someone showed you while they were explaining it, then you would be more likely to get it.*

The Main Thing:

That's kind of what Jesus was doing when He wrapped the towel around Him and took the basin to wash the disciples' feet. He had talked to them over and over about serving one another and caring for each other, but they just weren't getting it. He wanted them to see what that looked like acted out.

So, at this last meal together, Jesus picked up a towel and started caring for them by washing their feet. What did Jesus want to teach them? He wanted to teach them one last time that we should be willing to do anything to help someone—even if it's servant work. We should never consider ourselves too good to serve someone else.

- How do we serve each other today?

- Washing feet was a yucky job, but Jesus was willing to say, "I'll be the one to wash your feet."

- When we lend a helping hand to someone instead of playing video games, we are serving like Jesus said.

- When we clean up a mess on the floor that someone else dropped from their plate instead of waiting for someone else to do that, we are serving like Jesus said.

- When we calm a crying baby with our silly faces, we are serving the tired mother who just wants to get home, and we're serving like Jesus said.

Jesus wrapped a towel around his waist and washed feet. How can you serve like Him?

Serving Obstacles

Resources Needed:

- Basins
- Bucket of water
- Cups
- Items for an obstacle course

Resource Preparations:

- This is an outside game.
- Set up identical obstacle courses for each team.
- These can be chairs, traffic cones, hula hoops, or any other substantial object.
- Most people think of an obstacle course as objects that you go around, but don't forget that you can also include things that you climb over, go under, or crawl through.
- When the courses are ready, explain the path the players will take to get through them.

The Fun Stuff:

- Form teams of six players each.
- The object of this game is for each team to get six cups of water in their basin.
- Place the team cup and a bucket of water at the starting line for each team.
- At the end of the obstacle course will be the basin.
- The kids will dip their cup in the bucket and carry the water through the course, pouring it in the basin when they get to it.
- Then, they will return to their team where they will give the cup to the next player.
- The first team to get six cups of water in their basin wins.

The Main Thing:

Jesus taught His disciples about serving by wrapping a towel around His waist, grabbing a basin of water and washing their feet. Washing someone's feet was work that the servants did, because people wore sandals and their feet would be dirty when they entered the house. The disciples were well aware that this was a servant's job. But, Jesus did it anyway.

Say:

- Our game had an obstacle course, though.
- That was because serving others isn't always easy.

- It's not always going to go the way we thought it would.

- There are obstacles that we have to get around in order to serve someone.

- Some of those obstacles are in our attitudes toward certain people.

- Our own hearts and minds can be an obstacle.

- We must be willing to serve anyone, and sometimes that means working through our own inner obstacles.

- What other obstacles may we have to overcome in order to serve as the Lord expects?

Washcloth Handprint

Resources Needed:

- Fabric paint
- New washcloth
- Styrofoam™ plate

Resource Preparation:

- Place some fabric paint on the Styrofoam™ plate and smear it around until the paint covers most of the plate.

The Fun Stuff:

- Take the child's hand and press it into the paint. (Make sure the hand is totally flat and gets paint on every finger and the palm. Make sure the washcloth is on a hard surface and has no wrinkles in it.)
- Place the child's hand in position and press the palm down into the washcloth. Before moving, press on each finger. Lift the hand straight up so the paint will not smear.

The Main Thing:

Jesus took a towel and a basin of water, then proceeded to wash the feet of His disciples. He told the disciples that He was giving them an example of how they should treat one another. He told them that they would be blessed if they would become servants.

- This washcloth can serve as a reminder that Jesus washed His disciples' feet.
- But, even more than that, don't be afraid to get this washcloth dirty, because you are using it to serve others.
- When you help others, most of time you are using your hands.
- Your hands can give an encouraging pat, they can hold the hand of someone who is crying, they can pull weeds at someone's house while they are on vacation, or they can make cookies to take to someone moving onto your block.
- Find ways to use the washcloth that will help others.
- **Ask:**
  - Can you think of ways your washcloth could be used to help someone else?
  - Jesus wants you to be a servant, also.

Communion and the Last Supper

Matthew 26:26-29

Read the Scripture passage in whatever version you prefer. We have chosen NIV (New International Version), which we find more kid-friendly.

Bible Story

While they were eating, Jesus took bread, and when he had given thanks, he broke it and gave it to his disciples, saying, "Take and eat; this is my body."

Then he took a cup, and when he had given thanks, he gave it to them, saying, "Drink from it, all of you. This is my blood of the covenant, which is poured out for many for the forgiveness of sins. I tell you, I will not drink from this fruit of the vine from now on until that day when I drink it new with you in my Father's kingdom."

Key Element:

As a devout Jew, Jesus celebrated the Passover to remember how God had delivered the Israelites from their slavery in Egypt. This Passover meal-turned-Last Supper will commemorate God's new plan of deliverance. There is so much tradition that started during this meal. This is where the precious sacrament of communion began. The children are probably familiar with communion, but more than likely haven't connected the dots—between Passover, the Last Supper, and why we observe communion today. Teaching about the Last Supper and communion as an important part of Holy Week will help children understand more about the resurrection.

Making Haroseth

Resources Needed:

- Apples, diced
- Big bowl
- Brown sugar
- Cinnamon
- Copy of recipe for haroseth for each child to take home
- Honey
- Lemon juice
- Pecans, chopped
- Spoon

The Main Thing:

Talk about the Passover dishes and what each dish helped the Jewish people remember. Each dish represents part of the struggle and deliverance of the Israelites from their slavery in Egypt. Roasted lamb was the main course and represented the lamb that was killed and its blood sprinkled over the door so the Angel of Death would *pass over*. The bread was flat like a big cracker. (If you'd like to show the kids this bread, you can purchase matza bread in the cultural aisle of your grocery.) The Israelites were in a hurry to leave Egypt and did not have time to wait for the bread to rise, so they didn't put leavening in it. Bitter herbs reminded them of how awful it was to be slaves in Egypt. Green herbs dipped in saltwater were a reminder of all the salty tears that were shed during the time of slavery. Haroseth is a mixture of tasty ingredients that mimic the bricks and mortar the Israelites had to make in order to build the Egyptian buildings.

The Fun Stuff:

- The children will really enjoy making their own batch of haroseth.
- Give the children an experience they will long remember.
- Because the kids are familiar with all of the ingredients (and usually like each one), they will readily taste this dish.
- Don't be surprised when they ask for more!

Haroseth Recipe

4 lg. apples, finely diced
2 T. lemon juice (or orange juice)
½ c. chopped pecans (or another nut)
4 T. brown sugar
2 T. honey
1 t. cinnamon

- Place the diced apples in a bowl and sprinkle the lemon juice over them. Stir.

- The lemon juice will keep the apples from turning dark.

- Add all the other ingredients and stir. Enjoy!

- Get some condiment cups with lids to send a sample of the haroseth with the kids.

- Don't forget to include a copy of the recipe, because kids will want to make more at home.

It All Happened at Dinner?

Resources Needed:

- A 3-step stool
- Bowl of croutons
- Bucket of water
- Cup
- Empty bucket
- Small paper plate
- Spoon

Resource Preparations:

- Set up these 4 stations, but duplicate each station so two teams can play against one another.
  - First station: set the 3-step stool
  - Second station: place the bowl of croutons, the spoon and the plate on a table.
  - Third station: place the empty bucket, the bucket of water and the cup on a table.
  - Fourth station: needs no set-up.

The Fun Stuff:

- At the signal, one child from each team will run to his first station.
- He or she will climb the 3 steps on the stool and shout, "They went to a room upstairs."
- Then, the child will come down the 3 steps (make a point of telling the kids there will be no jumping off—every step must be used), and run to the second station.
- The child will dip the spoon into the croutons and put a spoonful on the plate.
- When she has done this, she will shout, "The disciples ate together!"
- Off the child goes to station three. Here the child will dip the cup in the bucket of water and pour the water into the empty bucket.
- The child will say, "Jesus washed their feet."
- The player will then run out the door and back in shouting, "Judas left!"
- If you have a room with two doors, then he or she can run out one and back in the other.

- When two players have completed the entire route, then give the signal for the next two kids to go.

- You can set as many of these courses up as you like and have more kids participating at the same time.

- It is important, though, that each team have its own course.

Make an Object Lesson

Resources Needed:

- Cupcake
- Flashlight
- Paint brush
- Pair of pruners
- Sunscreen
- Teddy bear
- Vegetable peeler
- Watering can

Resource Preparation:

- You can add to the list of objects above, or change them if you like, but they are suggestions to get you started.
- Place the objects where the children can see them. Then each child (or each small group) can choose an object, but don't tell them why.
- The children will explore the object—what it does, what it looks like, when it is used—and then create their own object lesson that will tell something about God.
- The easiest way to do this is for the children to finish this sentence about their object: This _____ (object) reminds me of God, because it _____.
- Then, let the kids share what they have come up with.

The Main Thing:

We don't have Jesus' sandals to remember Him by. We don't have a piece of furniture from His house. We don't have a cup that He drank out of, or a lock of His hair.

What Jesus left is something more special than having a "thing" that belonged to Him. He left us ways to remember Him in object lessons, using things we can touch and see and understand.

One of those ways to remember Him is communion. When we drink the juice and eat the bread, they are like object lessons that tell us something about what Jesus did for us. When we drink the juice, we remember that Jesus died on the cross, His blood was spilled to take the punishment for the ways we have disobeyed God. The bread reminds us that it was His body that was broken on the cross for each of us. The juice and the bread have a new meaning; they are an object lesson for us. Every time we see juice and bread, we remember what Jesus did on the cross for us.

Reminders

Resources Needed:

- Easter items (see list under Fun Stuff)**
- Paper
- Pencils
- Tray

Resource Preparations:

- There are smells that trigger personal memories for me.
- When I smell gasoline, I think of my dad because he owned service stations and always smelled like the gas he pumped.
- When I smell newly mowed grass, I want to go for ice cream, because when I was little, as soon as the yard work was done, we would hop in the truck and go for ice cream at Zesto.
- When I smell a kitchen where there has been a lot of frying and canning going on, I think of my great-grandmother's farmhouse, because it always smelled like that. She loved to work in her kitchen.
- Share some reminders from your own past and ask the children if they have anything to share.

The Fun Stuff:

Say: Let's see how well you can remember.

- Play the old game where some items are placed on the tray and the kids will look at them for 30 seconds.
- Then, they have to try to remember everything they saw and write the items down.
- **Place items on the tray that you see during Easter: marshmallow chick, jellybeans, plastic egg, fake grass, basket, dye kit, and other little knick-knacks that you can pick up at the dollar store.

The Main Thing:

Jesus gave us communion to remember Him by. He didn't give us a framed picture of Himself, but He gave us the meaning of the bread to help us remember what Jesus did on the cross. Even the smell of bread or the fruity juice can help you remember Jesus.

Set the Table

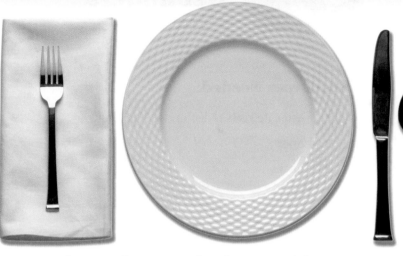

Resources Needed:

- Marker
- Paper cups
- Paper placemats
- Paper plates
- Plastic utensils

Resource Preparation:

- Beforehand, lay a full place setting on a paper placemat. Draw around each piece and then remove them.
- Do this 13 times, so there is a marked placemat for each person at the Last Supper. Lay these at one end of the room.
- Then, put the forks in one place (maybe on a counter), the plates in another place (maybe on a work table), the knives in another place (maybe on the windowsill), and so forth.

Ask:

- When do you share a meal with someone?
- Does your family get together at holidays or do friends come over on a Friday night?
- Talk about what you have to do to get ready for this special meal together.

The Fun Stuff:

- **Say:** For the Passover meal that Jesus and His disciples would share, the table had to be set for 13.
- Someone needed to put 13 place settings on the table to get ready for the Passover meal.
- When you set a table, there is a plate, glass, knife, fork, and spoon at each place setting. Let's play a little relay to set our table.
- The Bible says that Jesus sent two of the disciples ahead to make the preparations.
- **Directions:**
  o When you call out the names of two children, they will run around the room gathering up one fork, one knife, one spoon, one cup, and one plate. Then, they will take them to one of the placemats and put the pieces in the appropriate place.
  o Once one of the children is done, immediately call out the name of another child. Continue doing this until all 13 place settings are complete.

Share a Meal

Resources Needed:

- Ingredients for recipes you decide to use for the meal.

- See some recipes below.

Resource Preparation:

- This is the perfect time for kids to have the opportunity to serve others. They can provide a meal.

- Before you get crazy about having kids cooking in the kitchen, they really can do this. The trick is to have everything set up for them with ingredients and all the utensils they will need.

- Try to find recipes that just require items being poured together, such as those following:

Suggested Easy Recipes:

Fruit Salad

- Can of pears, mandarin oranges, pineapple chunks

- Blueberries, raspberries, bananas, blackberries

- Sugar or Splenda™

- The kids can use a regular table knife to slice the bananas and the pears.

- The rest of it is just pouring into a large bowl. Make sure you include the juice in the cans.

- Put sugar or Splenda™ on, as needed. Mix thoroughly. Spoon the fruit salad into small airtight containers.

Garden Vegetable Potato Salad

- 2 lbs. red potatoes

- 1 c. frozen peas, 1 c. corn kernels

- 1 large carrot, 1 c. broccoli, 4 green onions

- ¾ c. plain yogurt, ¾ c. mayonnaise

- 1 t. dill weed, ½ t. black pepper

- Beforehand, cook the whole potatoes by boiling them 15-20 minutes until fork tender.

- Slice the green onions because they are so small.

- The kids will slice the potatoes into bite-size chunks. They will also slice the carrot and chop the broccoli into small pieces.

- Combine the potatoes, peas, carrot, corn, broccoli, and onion in a bowl.
- Mix the yogurt, mayonnaise, dill and pepper together. Pour this over the mixed vegetables and stir until the vegetables are covered. Chill. (This makes about 12 servings.)

Hot Chicken Salad

- 2 cans of chicken, drained, 1 can cream of chicken soup
- ½ c. mayonnaise (not salad dressing)
- 5 boiled eggs, whites only, 2 T. lemon juice
- 1 c. cheese, 1 ½ c. crushed potato chips
- Combine the soup, mayonnaise and lemon juice in a casserole dish.
- Chop the boiled eggs in big pieces, setting the yolks aside for the dog.
- Crumble the chicken in the soup mixture and add the egg whites. Cover with the crushed potato chips and then sprinkle on the cheese.
- Bake at 350 degrees for 40 minutes uncovered.

The Fun Stuff:

- It is important that the children take the meal to the people they prepared it for.
- Arrange for them to deliver the meal to someone who is recovering from surgery (especially if it's a surgery on their leg, foot, or hip where it's difficult for them to walk, and yet they have no dietary restrictions).
- You could take the meal to an elderly couple or someone who is out of work.
- The kids really can do this, and you'll be amazed at the lasting impact it has on them. Giving them significant ways to serve at this age is critical for raising kids who will love to serve as adults.
- Include a note with the meal that says, "We learned about how Jesus shared a meal with His disciples and we wanted to share this meal with you."

The Main Thing:

The Bible tells us of many times when Jesus shared a meal with someone. Sometimes, the religious people weren't happy with Him because of who He chose to eat with, like Zacchaeus the tax collector. Jesus blessed the loaves and fish and shared a meal with 5,000 people. And now, one of the last things He does with His disciples is to share the Passover meal.

Peter's Promise

Matthew 26:31-35

Read the Scripture passage in whatever version you prefer. We have chosen NIV (New International Version), which we find more kid-friendly.

Bible Story

Then Jesus told them, "This very night you will all fall away on account of me, for it is written:

"'I will strike the shepherd, and the sheep of the flock will be scattered.' But after I have risen, I will go ahead of you into Galilee."

Peter replied, "Even if all fall away on account of you, I never will."

"Truly I tell you," Jesus answered, "this very night, before the rooster crows, you will disown me three times."

But Peter declared, "Even if I have to die with you, I will never disown you." And all the other disciples said the same.

Key Elements:

Each of us finds ourselves in Peter's promise of "to the death" commitment. Children will readily identify with Peter in this story. Just like Peter, they don't see anything that could possibly stand in their way, and at the moment they feel so strong. When we make this kind of promise, it really is beyond our imaginations to think we could ever do otherwise. It's important to make these wholehearted commitments. The children will learn about making big and important promises to follow God.

Balloon in a Bottle

Resources Needed:

- Balloon
- Empty water bottle

Resource Preparation:

- Water bottles come in a variety of sizes.
- The kids can see this a little better if you use the larger water bottle.

The Fun Stuff:

- Ask a volunteer if he can blow up the balloon. When he says that he can, ask if he is sure.
- Of course the volunteer is sure because he has blown up balloons many times before. So, let him blow up the balloon. Very good! Let the air back out of the balloon.
- Ask the volunteer if he can blow up the balloon a second time. When he says that he can, ask if he is sure. Of course he is sure, because he just blew it up.
- Then, pull out the empty water bottle and place the balloon into the bottle. Pull the neck completely around the opening into the bottle. When you hold the bottle now, the balloon should be hanging down inside the bottle. The volunteer will now try to blow up the balloon.

Ask:

- What happened? I thought you said you could blow up this balloon. You were so sure you could.

The Main Thing:

Sometimes we are sure that we can do something, but when the time comes, it's not as easy as we thought it was going to be. When Peter promised Jesus that he would never deny Jesus, Peter really truly thought that he would never deny Jesus. But when the time came, Peter couldn't do what he thought he could do.

Greased Eggplant

Resources Needed:

- Eggplant
- Vasoline™

Resource Preparation:

- For this activity, you want to be outside and you either want to cover the kids with a plastic bag smock or tell them to wear their worst clothes. We're going to get messy!

The Fun Stuff:

- Make the kids think that you are just doing a warm-up game before the messy game.
- In this relay we're going to see which team can get their eggplant to the goal first.
- The kids will spread out on a long grassy area, about ten feet apart, if possible (or further). The first person on the team will have an eggplant.
- At the signal, the first person will run to the second person and pass him or her the eggplant.
- The second person will take it to the third and so on until the eggplant gets to the last person.
- Now, ask the kids to promise that they will not drop the eggplant as they take it down their team line. You can even make them raise their hand and make it a formal promise.

Now, play this way.

- After they have successfully passed the eggplant the first time, ask them to make the promise again for this next round. After they have promised, bring out some helpers who will apply Vasoline™ all over each eggplant.
- As they pass it this time, they are sure to drop it several times and have a difficult time holding onto it. If you want to have some over-the-top crazy fun, use a small watermelon and do the same thing.

The Main Thing:

What was different the second time? We applied the Vasoline™ and the situation changed. It wasn't the same race you thought it was going to be. When Peter promised he would never deny Jesus, he based his promise on what he knew. Nothing he had experienced with Jesus so far gave him reason to think that he would deny Jesus. But, when the situation changed, Peter found it difficult to keep that promise.

Promise Race

Resource Needed:

- Hula Hoops™

The Fun Stuff:

- Divide the kids into teams of equal numbers (8-10 is good). Each team will form a chain by holding hands.

- Give the first person in each chain a Hula Hoop™.

- The object of the game is for everyone on each team to go through the Hula Hoop™ without letting go of the next person's hand. Each time a kid steps through the Hula Hoop™, he or she must say, "I promise to _____" and give a promise that he has made or one that she makes up.

The Main Thing:

Promises can be tricky, because we don't know if we can actually be strong enough to keep them if the circumstances change. Peter promised Jesus that he would never deny Him. The Bible quotes Peter as saying, "Even if I have to die with you, I will never say I don't know you." Peter really meant that promise, but when the circumstances got dangerous and scary, Peter didn't keep his promise. In our game, some of us were able to hold on even though it was difficult to go through the Hula Hoops™ this way, but others weren't able to hold on. We need to ask God to give us the strength we need to keep our promises.

Jesus Prays in Gethsemane

Mark 14:32-42

Read the Scripture passage in whatever version you prefer. We have chosen NIV (New International Version), which we find more kid-friendly.

Bible Story

They went to a place called Gethsemane, and Jesus said to his disciples, "Sit here while I pray." He took Peter, James and John along with him, and he began to be deeply distressed and troubled. "My soul is overwhelmed with sorrow to the point of death," he said to them. "Stay here and keep watch."

Going a little farther, he fell to the ground and prayed that if possible the hour might pass from him. "*Abba*, Father," he said, "everything is possible for you. Take this cup from me. Yet not what I will, but what you will."

Then he returned to his disciples and found them sleeping. "Simon," he said to Peter, "are you asleep? Couldn't you keep watch for one hour? Watch and pray so that you will not fall into temptation. The spirit is willing, but the flesh is weak."

Once more he went away and prayed the same thing. When he came back, he again found them sleeping, because their eyes were heavy. They did not know what to say to him.

Returning the third time, he said to them, "Are you still sleeping and resting? Enough! The hour has come. Look, the Son of Man is delivered into the hands of sinners. Rise! Let us go! Here comes my betrayer!"

Key Element:

It's interesting to note what Jesus was doing when He was arrested. He was praying. He was talking with His Heavenly Father. He was affirming His commitment to go through with God's plan. The children will learn that when life throws you troubles, the trouble needs to find you on your knees praying for God's leading. Jesus armed Himself with prayer, and the children will learn that they should do as Jesus did.

Garden of Gethsemane Rhyme

Preparation:

Teach the children this simple rhyme before you tell the story of Jesus going to the Garden of Gethsemane to pray. Go over it several times.

> **Why are you asleep?**
> **Can't you sit here and pray?**
> **I need you to be strong.**
> **This is an awful day.**

The Main Thing:

After they had shared the Passover meal together, Jesus took His disciples to the Garden of Gethsemane. He turned to them and told them to stay where they were and pray. Jesus took Peter, James, and John with Him further into the garden. Again, He turned to these three disciples and told them to stay there and pray, because He was deeply troubled.

Then, Jesus went on to pray by Himself. He knelt down on the ground and poured His heart out to God. He asked that if it was possible that He wouldn't have to go through what He knew waited for Him. But that wasn't all Jesus prayed. He also told God that He was willing to go through anything if it meant bringing people back to God.

After a while, Jesus came back to the disciples, but found them asleep. And He said,

> **Why are you asleep?**
> **Can't you sit here and pray?**
> **I need you to be strong.**
> **This is an awful day.**

Again, Jesus told them to stay there and pray while He went into the garden to be alone to pray. When He came out, again He found the disciples asleep. They just couldn't keep their eyes open! And, Jesus said,

> **Why are you asleep?**
> **Can't you sit here and pray?**
> **I need you to be strong.**
> **This is an awful day.**

A third time Jesus went further into the garden to pray by Himself, and a third time when He came out the disciples were asleep. And He said,

> **Why are you asleep?**
> **Can't you sit here and pray?**
> **I need you to be strong.**
> **This is an awful day.**

This time, though, He told them to get up because it was time for the one who would betray Him to do just that.

SCIENCE EXPERIMENT

It Should Be Easy

The Fun Stuff:

- Place a quarter on the floor about a foot away from the wall.

- Then, choose a child to stand between the wall and the quarter. He should have his feet together with his back and heels against the wall.

- Challenge him to pick up the coin without moving his feet.

- **Say:** It seems like a pretty easy thing to do, but the volunteer will fail. In order to pick up the coin, you have to change the way you are standing.

- Let's see how this little experiment with the quarter reminds us of something that happened to Jesus' disciples.

The Main Thing:

Jesus went into the Garden of Gethsemane to pray. He asked His disciples to pray with Him. That seemed like a pretty easy thing to do, didn't it? But each time Jesus came back to check on them, they had fallen asleep. They had failed. They should've been able to do it, but they just couldn't seem to keep their eyes open. They needed to change how they were approaching Jesus' request. I really believe that if they had understood the seriousness of what was about to happen, they would have changed how they sat in the garden to pray with Him. They would have found a way to stay awake.

Prayer Eggs

Resources Needed:

- Colorful lunch bags
- Copies of prayer slips
- Pencils
- Plastic eggs

Resource Preparations:

- Give each child a copy of the prayer strips and six plastic eggs.

  o *Dear Father, I don't want to act like I am ashamed to be one of Your followers. Help me not to be afraid when others ask me about You.*

  o *Dear Father, I want to give with a cheerful heart, and I want to give You everything. That's what You deserve.*

  o *Dear Father, help me to bear fruit and be all that You created me to be. I want others to know more about You because of how I live and what I say.*

  o *Dear Father, help me to love others as much as I love myself. No, Father, help me to love them more than I love myself. It will take Your strength to do that. You can remind me when I'm being selfish, when I need to think of others more.*

  o *Dear Father, if I had a palm branch I would wave it and shout, Hosanna! I want to celebrate Your gift to me every day of my life. Hosanna to my King!*

  o *Dear Father, help me to remember what You did for me when You sent Your Son, Jesus, to die on the cross and rise from the grave. When I see or taste the bread and the juice, I will stop all my other thoughts and be thankful.*

- They will cut their strips apart and roll them around a pencil to make it easier for them to stay inside a plastic egg.
- Provide colorful lunch bags for the kids to put their prayer eggs in.

The Main Thing:

When Jesus was in the Garden of Gethsemane, He poured out His heart to His Father in heaven. How awful it must have been to know that He was going to be nailed to a cross and killed. But still, Jesus prayed and willingly offered Himself to God's will.

Directions for the kids:

Say:

- Each day, pull out an egg and read the prayer on the slip. This is only a starter prayer. Each prayer has something to do with one of the stories that occurred during Holy Week.

- You can put the prayer strip back in your egg and return it to your bag after you've prayed, because these prayer eggs can be used over and over.

Judas Betrays Jesus

Mark 14:10-11, 43-50

Read the Scripture passage in whatever version you prefer. We have chosen NIV (New International Version), which we find more kid-friendly.

Bible Story

Then Judas Iscariot, one of the Twelve, went to the chief priests to betray Jesus to them. They were delighted to hear this and promised to give him money. So he watched for an opportunity to hand him over.

Just as he was speaking, Judas, one of the Twelve, appeared. With him was a crowd armed with swords and clubs, sent from the chief priests, the teachers of the law, and the elders.

Now the betrayer had arranged a signal with them: "The one I kiss is the man; arrest him and lead him away under guard." Going at once to Jesus, Judas said, "Rabbi!" and kissed him. The men seized Jesus and arrested him. Then one of those standing near drew his sword and struck the servant of the high priest, cutting off his ear.

"Am I leading a rebellion," said Jesus, "that you have come out with swords and clubs to capture me? Every day I was with you, teaching in the temple courts, and you did not arrest me. But the Scriptures must be fulfilled." Then everyone deserted him and fled.

Key Element:

Jesus, the One who had never sinned, still had a close friend who turned against Him. Although the children understand betrayal, it's on such a small scale compared to this. The children will be aware of the hurt that comes from a loved one's betrayal, but also understand that the heartache Jesus must have experienced was on an even grander scale.

Jellybean Dart Blower

Resources Needed:

- 5 copies of soldier
- 5 empty water bottles
- 18" length of ½" PVC
- Bucket of warm, soapy water
- Jellybeans
- Tape

Resource Preparations:

- Make copies of the soldier clip art provided in Appendix 9 and cut them out.
- Tape each one to an empty water bottle.
- Set up the water bottles about 3" apart in a row.

The Main Thing:

When Judas came to Jesus, he brought a band of soldiers with him and some other people who were after Jesus. Jesus had the power to fight against the soldiers. He could have caused them all to fall asleep, or He could have made them all get sick at their stomachs. He even could have made them all drop over dead! After all, Jesus had the power to raise Lazarus from the grave and to calm an angry sea with just a word. He could have taken care of those soldiers!

The Fun Stuff:

- On his or her turn, each child will hold the 18" piece of PVC out from his face, parallel to the ground.
- She will place a jellybean in the end of the PVC that is closest to her, take a big breath (not while her mouth is against the PVC) and aim at one of those soldiers.
- Then, have her blow into the PVC and see if she can shoot that jellybean at the soldier and make him fall down.
- Stick the end of the PVC that was in the child's mouth down in the warm soapy water and then dry it off.
- It's best to have several of the pipes ready, so the kids aren't waiting on each other.

More Main Thing:

Even though Jesus knew He had the power to do this to the soldiers, He didn't. He knew that what He would go through was part of God's plan and He willingly went with Judas and the soldiers.

The Kiss that Was Different

Resources Needed:

- Candy Hugs
- Candy Kisses
- Plastic eggs

Resource Preparations:

- Kids love to hunt for eggs, but be ready for a little twist. Place a candy Kiss in each of the plastic eggs and one candy Hug in one egg.
- It doesn't matter how many Kiss eggs you use; in fact, the more the better.
- Hide all the eggs and then send the children out to find them.
- Instruct them not to open the eggs, because they'll do that later once all the eggs have been found.

The Fun Stuff:

- Open one egg in front of the kids (one that you're sure has a Kiss in it). What's in here? It's a candy Kiss … yummy! Let me tell you that all the eggs have a chocolate Kiss in them, except one. It has something suspiciously like the Kiss in it, but not quite. When you are chosen, you will be asked if you think you have one of the real Kisses. If you are right, then you'll get to keep the Kiss. Remember, all of the eggs have Kisses in them, except that one.
- Choose one child at a time and ask her if she thinks she has a Kiss. Most of the children will guess that they have a Kiss, and more than likely, the person with the Hug will also say she thinks she has a Kiss. Once the person with the Hug candy in her egg is found, then tell all the other kids they can now open their eggs and get their Kiss out.
- Hold up a Kiss and a Hug, side-by-side.
- **Say:** These look an awful lot alike. It would be easy to mistake this Hug for a Kiss if you weren't looking closely, especially if it was mixed up in a bowl of Kisses.

The Main Thing:

That reminds me of how Judas used a kiss, and not a chocolate one, as a signal to point out Jesus to the people who were after Him. Judas was one of the disciples! He was one of the twelve special men who were with Jesus almost all the time! Just like our Hug looked an awful lot like the Kiss, Judas looked an awful lot like the people who were faithful followers of Jesus. No one would have thought Judas would have been the one to hand Jesus over. The people of that day greeted each other with a kiss on the cheek. That was the ordinary thing to do, and everyone expected it. So, for Judas to kiss Jesus when he walked up to Jesus in the Garden of Gethsemane would have been a normal thing to do. It would've looked like any other kiss. That kiss was like all the others…or was it? Just like there is just a little something different in the Hug that makes it different than the candy Kiss, the kiss that Judas gave Jesus that day was just a little different. It was not a kiss of warmth and greeting; it was a kiss of betrayal.

Who Betrayed Jesus?

Resources Needed:

- 12 index cards
- Beanbags
- Masking tape

Resource Preparations:

- Write the name of one of the disciples on each of the 12 index cards:
  - Peter
  - Andrew
  - James
  - John
  - Philip
  - Bartholomew
  - Matthew
  - Thomas
  - Judas Iscariot
  - Judas, son of James
  - Simon, the Zealot
  - James, son of Alphaeus
- Use the masking tape to make a grid, 4 by 3, with each of the boxes being about an 8" square. This doesn't have to be exact.
- The further away you plan on tossing, the larger the boxes should be.
- Tape one index card face down in each of the squares.
- Then, mark a stand-behind line about 8 feet back from the grid.

The Fun Stuff:

- The kids will take turns tossing a beanbag at the grid.

- If the beanbag lands on a square, then turn over the card and ask, "Did this disciple betray Jesus?"

- If the child is correct, remove the card and give the child 100 points.

- It gets more difficult as you go, because the only way you can earn points is to land on a square that still has an index card on it.

- Once someone lands on the Judas Iscariot square and identifies him as the disciple who betrayed Jesus, the game is over.

- See who has the most points.

(The grid can be duplicated to accommodate more children.)

Peter's Denial

Luke 22:54-62

Read the Scripture passage in whatever version you prefer. We have chosen NIV (New International Version), which we find more kid-friendly.

Bible Story

Then seizing him, they led him away and took him into the house of the high priest. Peter followed at a distance. And when some there had kindled a fire in the middle of the courtyard and had sat down together, Peter sat down with them. A servant girl saw him seated there in the firelight. She looked closely at him and said, "This man was with him."

But he denied it. "Woman, I don't know him," he said.

A little later someone else saw him and said, "You also are one of them."

"Man, I am not!" Peter replied.

About an hour later another asserted, "Certainly this fellow was with him, for he is a Galilean."

Peter replied, "Man, I don't know what you're talking about!" Just as he was speaking, the rooster crowed. The Lord turned and looked straight at Peter. Then Peter remembered the word the Lord had spoken to him: "Before the rooster crows today, you will disown me three times." And he went outside and wept bitterly.

Key Element:

We have the best of intentions when we voice our devotion, but fear is the enemy and does nasty things to our commitment. Oh Peter! What were you thinking?

We're disappointed in Peter, and yet we relate to how frightened he must have been as he found himself in the middle of a scene that would literally change history. The yo-yo that was Peter's commitment and his denial is something that adults and children can easily identify with. Peter was convicted of what he had done...immediately. The children will learn that we are also guilty of trying to hide our belief in Jesus Christ.

Little Dyed Chick

Resource Needed:

- A little dyed chick

Resource Preparation:

- During the Easter season, pet stores often have little chicks that have been dyed all different colors.

- Ask a pet store if you can borrow one for the day or purchase one if you know where it can have a home afterwards.

- Or, if you're really adventurous, take the kids on a field trip to the pet store.

- There are pink and blue and green and yellow little chicks…all dyed to be a festive spring addition to the Easter celebration.

- Those aren't the colors they are supposed to be, though; the chicks are in their Easter disguise. What happens when the little chick grows up? Is he still the dyed color?

- No, he looks like God created him to look. He looks like a real chicken, not a dyed one.

The Main Thing:

Peter wanted to know what was going on when they arrested Jesus, but Peter didn't want anyone to identify him as one of Jesus' followers. He tried to stay disguised. He wasn't being the man of God that he was supposed to be. When it was all over and Jesus had gone back to heaven, Peter's true colors came out. He no longer wanted to stay hidden as a follower of Jesus. Because Peter stopped hiding, he became the man God meant him to be, and was the one who helped start the church. When Peter grew up in his belief and understanding of Jesus, he was God's man…with no disguises.

No, Not Me!

Resources Needed:

- 2 plastic eggs
- Candy-coated chocolate candies

Resource Preparations:

- Beforehand, prepare the plastic eggs by putting three chocolate candies inside.

- **Say:** We're going to play a game with a plastic egg to remind us about this story.

- The children will sit in a circle.

- Choose one child to stand in the middle and close his eyes.

- The children will pass around one plastic egg behind their backs. When the person in the middle crows, the egg stops.

- The person in the middle then has to count to three before opening his eyes.

- He will then try to choose who has the egg. If he chooses wrong, the person he chose will say, "No, not me!"

- Keep choosing until the person with the egg is found.

- The person holding the egg gets to open it and eat the three chocolate candies, but he or she also gets to be the next rooster in the middle.

- (You could have other filled eggs as prizes for anyone who actually finds the egg on the first choosing.)

- Start another egg around in the same manner. While that egg is being passed around, the one that was emptied on the last round can be refilled.

The Main Thing:

Peter told three different people that he didn't know Jesus. Why would he do such a thing? (Because he was afraid they might hurt him like they were hurting Jesus.) What did Peter say each time someone asked, "Aren't you the one who was with him?" Peter said, "No, not me!"

Peter Denies Christ

Directions:

Teach the children this little response. Three times during the story, they will repeat the response as part of the storyline.

I don't know Him. I don't know Him.

He is NOT my friend!

The Main Thing:

At the Last Supper, just a few hours before, Peter said that he would never leave Jesus. Jesus knew what was about to happen and he said to Peter, "This night, before the rooster crows three times you will tell other people that you don't know Me." (*Can you make the sound a rooster makes? Flap your wings and crow when I give the signal.*)

Later on that evening, when Jesus was arrested, Peter hid behind doorways (*move behind something and peer out*) and covered his face (*bring your arm up over your face*) as he tried to see what was happening to Jesus. A young girl came up to Peter and said, "Aren't you one of His disciples?" Peter was afraid someone might arrest him too if they knew that he was one of Jesus' disciples, so he said,

(*Point to children to say*)

I don't know Him. I don't know Him.

He is NOT my friend!

Then, Peter walked over to the fire to warm his hands. (*Rub your hands together to warm them.*) There were other men around the fire talking with one another. One of the men spoke to Peter and said, "Aren't you one of His disciples?" Fear swept over Peter again and he said,

(*Point to children to say*)

I don't know Him. I don't know Him.

He is NOT my friend!

A soldier was standing nearby who had also been in the Garden of Gethsemane when Jesus was arrested. Peter had been in the garden, and the soldier said, "I saw you in the garden with Jesus! You are with Him!" Immediately, Peter yelled at the soldier,

(*Point to children to say*)

I don't know Him. I don't know Him.

He is NOT my friend!

Over the noise of the courtyard Peter heard a rooster crow. (*Tell the children to make their wings and crow.*) It reminded him of the words Jesus had said, "This night, before the rooster crows, three times you will tell other people that you don't know me." As Jesus walked past Peter, He looked at him sadly. Peter rushed away from the courtyard and away from Jesus to find a place where he could cry. (*Rub your eyes.*) He was so sad that he had disappointed Jesus.

What did Peter say when the servant girl recognized him as a friend of Jesus?

(*Children say:*)

I don't know Him. I don't know Him.

He is NOT my friend.

What did Peter say when the man at the fire recognized him as a friend of Jesus?

(*Children say:*)

I don't know Him. I don't know Him.

He is NOT my friend.

What did Peter say when the soldier recognized him as being a friend of Jesus?

(*Children say:*)

I don't know Him. I don't know Him.

He is NOT my friend.

Going Deeper:

- Peter had disappointed Jesus. What do we do that makes Jesus sad?
- Instruct the children to crow each time you mention something that would make Jesus sad.

   o   lie to your parents

   o   call someone a name

   o   laugh at a silly game

   o   smack someone

   o   invite someone to church

   o   pout

   o   refuse to help out

   o   sing a song

   o   give someone a hug

   o   have a bad attitude

- The rooster crowing pointed out to Peter that he had disappointed Jesus and made Jesus sad. We need to pay attention to our actions and our words so we don't do or say something that would make Jesus sad.

Strut Like a Rooster

Resources Needed:

- 2 concrete blocks
- Balance beam
- Cardstock
- Rooster cards

Resource Preparations:

- A 4" x 4" x 8' beam works great for a balance beam. To make it even nicer, cover it with several coats of polyurethane. If you do this, the kids will be able to walk on the balance beam without fear of splinters. Elevate the balance beam with two concrete blocks. This will raise it high enough that kids feel like they're up in the air, but not so high that they'll hurt themselves if they lose their balance. (Put the effort into making these beams nice and they will serve you in a multitude of ways through the years!)

- Make a set of 16 rooster cards. Run a copy of the rooster clip art (Appendix 8) and place the rooster in the four quadrants of a piece of cardstock. Make four copies, so when cut apart, you'll have 16 cards.

- Write each question below on the back of a rooster card, and then you'll also have four that will be blank.

- Place all the cards face down (only the roosters are showing) on the ground right off one end of the balance beam.

The Fun Stuff:

- Where does a rooster sit when he is crowing? He usually sits on a fence.

- As he crows, he walks up and down the top of the fence. Some people say that the rooster is strutting when he walks the fence.

- We're going to pretend this balance beam is a rooster's fence and we're the roosters strutting.

- The kids will take turns strutting across the balance beam, picking up a rooster card, and then returning back across the beam with the card in hand.

- If the card has a question on it, ask the child to give their answer. If they don't know the answer, let them choose a friend to help them. If the card is blank, they don't have to do anything.

Questions for the Rooster Cards:

- Jesus was arrested and taken to the house of the high _____.

- How many times did Peter say he didn't know Jesus?

- When the rooster crowed, Jesus turned and _____ at Peter.

- Peter sat near a _____ in the yard to warm himself.

- Who was the disciple who said he didn't know Jesus?

- Was it a young girl or a boy who said, "Aren't you one of His disciples?"

- When Peter heard the rooster crow, he left and _____ really hard.

- What bird was it that made his sound when Peter said he didn't know who Jesus was?

- Why do you think Peter said he didn't know Jesus?

- Why did Peter feel so bad when he heard the rooster crow?

Jesus' Trial Before Pilate

Matthew 27:11-26

Read the Scripture passage in whatever version you prefer. We have chosen NIV (New International Version), which we find more kid-friendly.

Bible Story

Meanwhile Jesus stood before the governor, and the governor asked him, "Are you the king of the Jews?"

"You have said so," Jesus replied.

When he was accused by the chief priests and the elders, he gave no answer. Then Pilate asked him, "Don't you hear the testimony they are bringing against you?" But Jesus made no reply, not even to a single charge—to the great amazement of the governor.

Now it was the governor's custom at the festival to release a prisoner chosen by the crowd. At that time they had a well-known prisoner whose name was Jesus Barabbas. So when the crowd had gathered, Pilate asked them, "Which one do you want me to release to you: Jesus Barabbas, or Jesus who is called the Messiah?" For he knew it was out of self-interest that they had handed Jesus over to him.

While Pilate was sitting on the judge's seat, his wife sent him this message: "Don't have anything to do with that innocent man, for I have suffered a great deal today in a dream because of him."

But the chief priests and the elders persuaded the crowd to ask for Barabbas and to have Jesus executed.

"Which of the two do you want me to release to you?" asked the governor.

"Barabbas," they answered.

"What shall I do, then, with Jesus who is called the Messiah?" Pilate asked.

They all answered, "Crucify him!"

"Why? What crime has he committed?" asked Pilate.

But they shouted all the louder, "Crucify him!"

When Pilate saw that he was getting nowhere, but that instead an uproar was starting, he took water and washed his hands in front of the crowd. "I am innocent of this man's blood," he said. "It is your responsibility!"

All the people answered, "His blood is on us and on our children!"

Then he released Barabbas to them. But he had Jesus flogged, and handed him over to be crucified.

Key Elements:

This was absolutely unbelievable! Those who had followed Jesus around the countryside and by the sea had to have been stunned by what was happening. The children will learn how absurd the accusations and the trial before Pilate really was. Choosing to have a known criminal released and a man put to death whose only crime was teaching about the Kingdom of God sounds beyond ridiculous now.

Collapsing Can

Resources Needed:

- Empty pop can
- Full pop can

The Fun Stuff:

- Set the full pop can on the floor and choose a child to stand on the can.
- Choose an older child or an adult to get down on the floor next to the can. The person on the floor will give the side of the can a good flick with their index finger.
- Warn them to flick and pull their hand away immediately. What happened? Nothing.

The Main Thing:

As long as the disciples were traveling around the countryside with Jesus and listening to Him teach, they felt pretty confident in their world. Everything was good when they were with Jesus. They were standing on sturdy ground, just like standing on this full pop can.

The Fun Stuff:

- Now, set the empty pop can on the floor and have the same child stand on it. The same person will be on the floor to flick the can. Repeat the warning to flick and pull your hand away quickly.
- As soon as the can is flicked it will collapse with a pop...and I mean the second it is touched. (If you don't get your hand away quickly enough it could pinch a little.)

More Main Thing:

When Jesus was arrested, the disciples' world seemed to collapse, just like our can collapsed. Everything was falling apart. The person they had devoted their lives to the last three years was now arrested and in a lot of trouble. Would Jesus ever come back to them? It didn't look like He would.

The Crowd

Resources Needed:

- Brown paper lunch bags
- Glue sticks
- Old magazines
- Scissors

The Main Thing:

Pilate really didn't want to sentence Jesus to the cross. He had a thought. It was the custom that one prisoner be released during Passover. He would give the crowd of people who had assembled a choice between releasing Jesus and releasing a well-known criminal named Barabbas.

When Pilate stood both Jesus and Barabbas before the angry mob of people, he asked them which of the men they would like to have freed. The people yelled, "Barabbas! Barabbas!" Then, Pilate asked them what he should do with Jesus. The crowd yelled back, "Crucify Him! Crucify Him!"

The Fun Stuff:

Say: *Let's make the crowd of people who gathered there to make their choice. We'll make them out of brown lunch sacks.*

- Each child will cut out a set of eyes, a nose, and a mouth from different faces they find in the old magazines. They should not use the features from the same photograph.
- The features will be out of proportion with one another, but that's the fun of this activity.
- The kids will cut off the top of the sack down to wherever they would like. They can fringe the top to make it look like hair, or cut strips and curl them. They might even want to try braiding the strips of paper sack.
- Glue the eyes, nose and mouth in place and you've got one of the people who was yelling in the crowd the day Pilate gave the people a choice.

The Crucifixion

Matthew 27:27-56

Read the Scripture passage in whatever version you prefer. We have chosen NIV (New International Version), which we find more kid-friendly.

Bible Story

Then the governor's soldiers took Jesus into the Praetorium and gathered the whole company of soldiers around him. They stripped him and put a scarlet robe on him, and then twisted together a crown of thorns and set it on his head. They put a staff in his right hand and knelt in front of him and mocked him. "Hail, king of the Jews!" they said. They spit on him, and took the staff and struck him on the head again and again. After they had mocked him, they took off the robe and put his own clothes on him. Then they led him away to crucify him.

As they were going out, they met a man from Cyrene, named Simon, and they forced him to carry the cross. They came to a place called Golgotha (which means The Place of the Skull). There they offered Jesus wine to drink, mixed with gall; but after tasting it, he refused to drink it. When they had crucified him, they divided up his clothes by casting lots. And sitting down, they kept watch over him there. Above his head they placed the written charge against him: THIS IS JESUS, THE KING OF THE JEWS. Two robbers were crucified with him, one on his right and one on his left. Those who passed by hurled insults at him, shaking their heads and saying, "You who are going to destroy the temple and build it in three days, save yourself! Come down from the cross, if you are the Son of God!"

In the same way the chief priests, the teachers of the law and the elders mocked him. "He saved others," they said, "but he can't save himself! He's the King of Israel! Let him come down now from the cross, and we will believe in him. He trusts in God. Let God rescue him now if he wants him, for he said, 'I am the Son of God.'" In the same way the robbers who were crucified with him also heaped insults on him.

From the sixth hour until the ninth hour darkness came over all the land. About the ninth hour Jesus cried out in a loud voice, "Eloi, Eloi, lama sabachthani?" which means, "My God, my God, why have you forsaken me?"

When some of those standing there heard this, they said, "He's calling Elijah."

Immediately one of them ran and got a sponge. He filled it with wine vinegar, put it on a stick, and offered it to Jesus to drink. The rest said, "Now leave him alone. Let's see if Elijah comes to save him."

And when Jesus had cried out again in a loud voice, he gave up his spirit.

At that moment the curtain of the temple was torn in two from top to bottom. The earth shook and the rocks split. The tombs broke open and the bodies of many holy people who had died were raised to life. They came out of the tombs, and after Jesus' resurrection they went into the holy city and appeared to many people.

When the centurion and those with him who were guarding Jesus saw the earthquake and all that had happened, they were terrified, and exclaimed, "Surely he was the Son of God!"

Many women were there, watching from a distance. They had followed Jesus from Galilee to care for his needs. Among them were Mary Magdalene, Mary the mother of James and Joses, and the mother of Zebedee's sons.

Key Elements:

Jesus' cruel death on the cross is an important concept for the children to understand. The suffering that He endured on the cross was our punishment for disobeying God. Our personal punishment should be just as severe. The children will learn that the cross is an important part of their faith in Christ, but nothing without what comes next.

SNACK

Crown of Thorns

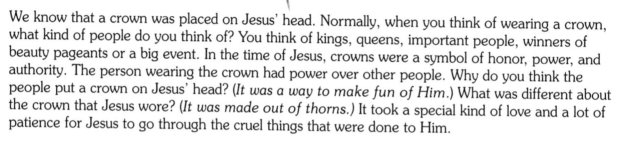

Resources Needed:

- Canned, refrigerated breadsticks (enough for each child to have one)
- Cookie sheet
- Knife
- Oven
- Plastic knives
- Toothpicks
- Waxed paper

The Main Thing:

We know that a crown was placed on Jesus' head. Normally, when you think of wearing a crown, what kind of people do you think of? You think of kings, queens, important people, winners of beauty pageants or a big event. In the time of Jesus, crowns were a symbol of honor, power, and authority. The person wearing the crown had power over other people. Why do you think the people put a crown on Jesus' head? (*It was a way to make fun of Him.*) What was different about the crown that Jesus wore? (*It was made out of thorns.*) It took a special kind of love and a lot of patience for Jesus to go through the cruel things that were done to Him.

The Fun Stuff:

- **Say:** *Let's make a special bread that will remind us of the crown of thorns.*
- Give each child a piece of waxed paper and one complete breadstick from a can of dough.
- The kids will use a plastic knife to cut the breadstick lengthwise into three long strips.
- Very gently, stretch the strips a little longer.
- Take the ends of all three strips and press them together onto the waxed paper. Now braid the strips. When the braiding is finished, bring the ends around to make a circle and press the dough together.
- Transfer the bread ring to a cookie sheet and bake according to the directions on the can.
- After the braided bread ring is baked, break toothpicks in half and stick them into the bread to make the thorns.

More Main Thing:

If you were the only person in the world, Jesus would have come to take your punishment. Think of the things you have done that have displeased God—ways that you failed to show Him your love. Look at the toothpick thorns that are in your bread, and think of each one as representing one of those times. Hopefully, you have accepted God's love and have asked Him to forgive you. That's why Jesus did all this…just for you!

The children may now eat their crown of thorns (first remove the toothpicks), or take it home to share the lesson with their family.

Floral Cross

Resources Needed:

- Artificial flowers
- Blocks of floral foam
- Pieces of 1" x 4" boards
- Thin floral wire
- Wire cutters

Resource Preparations:

- Recruit someone who is handy with wood to make a cross out of 1" x 4" boards. This can be any size, but I suggest that you make it at least 5 feet tall with a 3-foot crossbeam. Cover the cross with blocks of floral foam by wiring them around the wooden cross.

- Instead of purchasing artificial flowers for this, ask people to donate flowers from old arrangements, check out thrift stores, look at rummage sales, and ask at cemeteries. (Cemeteries collect all the arrangements left on the plots several times a year and usually dispose of them on the back of the property in a huge pile.)

- Beforehand, use wire cutters to cut the stems of the artificial flowers to about three inches. The children will poke the flowers into the floral foam until the cross is completely covered.

The Fun Stuff:

- Make this the week before Easter.

- Displaying this beautiful cross would be a wonderful way for the children to contribute to your church's Resurrection Sunday celebration.

The Main Thing:

Jesus was hung on a rough wood cross. Before we put the flowers on our cross, it wasn't very pretty. But, Jesus made His cross something beautiful, because He was there out of His huge love for each and every one of us. When Jesus rose from the grave, He made His sacrifice on the cross beautiful for all of us. Our flowers turned our cross into something really pretty that makes us smile. Every time you look at our changed cross, think about how Jesus made it possible for each of our lives to be changed.

Sign for the Cross

Resources Needed:

- Markers
- Rectangular piece of cardboard for each child

The Main Thing:

The Bible tells us that the soldiers made a sign to hang on the cross over Jesus' head. It was their way of making fun of Jesus. If you had the chance to make a sign that told other people who you think Jesus is, what would it say?

The Fun Stuff:

Give each child a rectangular piece of cardboard and some markers, so they can make their own sign to tell others who Jesus is.

Jesus is my savior

Standing Cross

Resources Needed:

- Craft sticks - both regular length and short ones
- Green tissue paper
- Hot glue gun
- Purple ribbon
- Styrofoam™ ice cream cups
- White glue

Resource Preparations:

- Beforehand, use a hot glue gun to make crosses out of the craft sticks. The shorter craft stick will be the crossbeam.
- Cut the green tissue paper into a little less than 1-inch squares.

The Fun Stuff:

- The children will take a piece of purple ribbon and drape it across the crossbeam of their craft stick cross. Glue it in a couple of places so it won't fall off.
- Turn the Styrofoam™ ice cream cup upside down.
- Wad up individual pieces of tissue paper and glue them onto the cup. Completely cover the outside of the cup.
- Poke the base of the cross through the center of the bottom of the cup. (Remember, it is upside down.) This will make the cross stand up.

The Blood of Jesus

Resources Needed:

- Paper towel
- Red permanent marker
- Spray bottle
- Whiteboard cleaner
- White construction paper

Resource Preparation:

- You will need a whiteboard cleaner that removes permanent marker.
- Pour it into the spray bottle.
- Wrap a piece of white construction paper around the spray bottle and write "Blood of Jesus" on the wrapper.

The Main Thing:

Ask: *What kind of things could we do or say that would be considered disobeying God?* (Let the children give their answers.)

- These things have a special word to describe them and that is "sin." (Pick up the red **permanent** marker and write SIN on the whiteboard.)

- And, how do we get rid of sin? Can we just think good thoughts and do something nice for someone? (Try to wipe SIN off the whiteboard using the paper towel.)

- Oh no! It's not coming off! I must have used a permanent marker. When we disobey God and sin against Him, then there's nothing we can do to make that go away completely.

- Oh wait! Here's a spray bottle. Let's see if maybe there's something in this bottle that will help.

- Spray the SIN with the spray bottle marked "Blood of Jesus" and then turn your back to it, as if you're going on with your teaching. Let it sit for a few seconds. The red ink from the marker will start bleeding and making streaks down the whiteboard.

- The kids will probably notice what's happening to SIN, but if not, turn around and make a point of noticing. What does that look like? It looks like blood, doesn't it?

- Look at the label on the spray bottle and then show it to the kids. That makes sense now, because this is a bottle of the Blood of Jesus.

- Now, use the paper towel to wipe SIN off the board.

- **Say:** When Jesus went to the cross, it wasn't because *He* had done something wrong. It was because *we* had done something wrong. *We* were the ones who deserved to be punished for disobeying God. He took the punishment that we deserve, and He paid for our sin with His own blood. God loved everyone He had created so much that He provided a way for all of us to come back to Him, if we will only accept the gift His only Son, Jesus, gave us.

- This was not really the Blood of Jesus, but it was a great way to help us understand what Jesus did for us by going to the cross.

The Burial

Matthew 27:57-66

Read the Scripture passage in whatever version you prefer. We have chosen NIV (New International Version), which we find more kid-friendly.

Bible Story

As evening approached, there came a rich man from Arimathea, named Joseph, who had himself become a disciple of Jesus. Going to Pilate, he asked for Jesus' body, and Pilate ordered that it be given to him. Joseph took the body, wrapped it in a clean linen cloth, and placed it in his own new tomb that he had cut out of the rock. He rolled a big stone in front of the entrance to the tomb and went away. Mary Magdalene and the other Mary were sitting there opposite the tomb.

The next day, the one after Preparation Day, the chief priests and the Pharisees went to Pilate. "Sir," they said, "we remember that while he was still alive that deceiver said, 'After three days I will rise again.' So give the order for the tomb to be made secure until the third day. Otherwise, his disciples may come and steal the body and tell the people that he has been raised from the dead. This last deception will be worse than the first."

"Take a guard," Pilate answered. "Go, make the tomb as secure as you know how. So they went and made the tomb secure by putting a seal on the stone and posting the guard.

Key Elements:

Anyone who has ever buried a loved one has a glimpse into the devastation that the followers of Jesus were going through as the stone was rolled across the entrance to the tomb. Where was their hope? Where was their future? It seemed to have died along with Jesus. The children will learn about the customs of burial to help them understand what happened. They will also get a sense of the loss that the disciples and other followers must have felt.

Extinguish the Flame

Resources Needed:

- Candles
- Dishes of sand
- Matches
- Rope
- Squirt gun

The Main Thing:

Mary, the disciples, and many other people who had followed Jesus and listened to Him teach about the kingdom of God, watched as He died on the cross. They had so much hope in this man who taught them about God. And now, He was dead. He was buried. Their light had gone out.

- How do you think they felt?
- What do you think was going through their minds?
- Where do you think they went when they saw that Jesus had been buried?

We're going to play a game to remind us of this story. (You'll probably want to go outside for this.)

The Fun Stuff:

- Place a candle for each person in a dish of sand, and set the dish on a table.
- Lay a rope in the grass to mark a stand-behind line. The distance from the rope to the candle is determined by the strength of your squirt gun.
- Light the candles.
- For each candle and squirt gun you have, choose a player.
- At the signal, the players will run to the stand-behind line and squirt at the flame on their candle.
- As soon as their candle is out, they must return with the squirt gun to the starting line.
- Relight the candles and send more players to squirt.

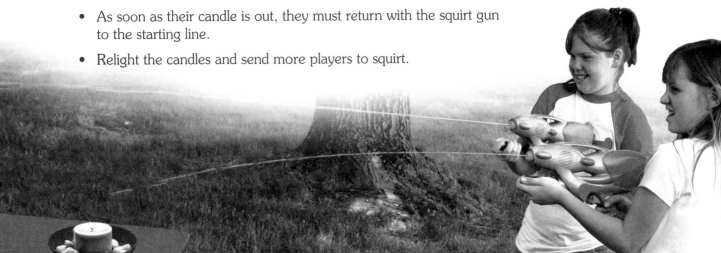

Flower Garden

Resources Needed:

- 2 bright colors of fun foam per child
- Ballpoint pens
- Green construction paper
- One-half of a plastic egg per child
- Sand
- Scissors
- Snack bags
- Tape
- Toilet paper roller per child

The Fun Stuff:

- Cover the toilet paper roller with a piece of green construction paper.
- Cut two 7" circles from the fun foam. In the middle of each 7" circle, draw around the end of the toilet paper roller. Cut these center circles out. Be careful not to make these circles any bigger than what you have drawn; in fact, you can go inside the line to make the circle a bit smaller than drawn.
- Use a ballpoint pen to draw petals on this 7" circle. The ends of the petals will go all the way out to the edge of the circle and then loop in to about ½" from the open circle in the middle.
- Stand the green toilet paper roller on end. Push the two fun foam flowers down over the roller. Position them so the petals are not on top of one another, but look like two layers of petals.
- Glue one side of a plastic egg onto the end of the roller to make the center of the flower.
- Put a couple of spoons of sand in a snack bag and zip it shut. Insert these at the base of each cardboard roller flower stem to make them more stable for standing.

The Main Thing:

Jesus was placed in a borrowed tomb. The tomb actually belonged to a wealthy man named Joseph of Arimethea. People who could afford it, purchased a plot of land and prepared their tomb for the day their family would need it. Most people who were hung on a cross did not have a place to be buried. This was probably a nice place with a small garden around it. A few wild flowers may have been growing here and there.

Even though the day was very sad and sorrowful as Joseph of Arimethea laid Jesus' body in the tomb, my imagination tells me that there probably were some dainty flowers there also to lend their beauty to a terrible situation.

Potpourri Ornament

Resources Needed:

- 2 buckets
- Bowl
- Glue gun
- Liquid starch
- Pastel yarns
- Plastic table covering
- Potpourri
- Round balloon
- Ruler
- Scissors

Resource Preparations:

- Before you start, make sure the work surface is covered with a plastic table covering.
- Blow up the balloon to the size you want your ornament. (You could also use water balloons.)
- Turn your buckets over and rest the ruler between them.
- Tie one end of a piece of yarn around the knot of the balloon and the other end around the ruler, so the balloon is suspended in the air.

The Fun Stuff:

- Cut the yarn into manageable lengths (30" – 45").
- Put a good amount of the liquid starch in the bowl. Pull the yarn through the liquid starch until the entire piece of yarn is wet. Then, wrap it around the balloon. Keep wrapping pieces of yarn around the balloon until there are just small holes showing through to the balloon.
- Let the balloon hang there at least overnight. You want it to be completely dry, so don't get impatient.
- When it's dry, gently pop the balloon. Choose a point on the balloon to be the top of your ornament. Clip a piece of yarn (or two, if necessary) to make a hole big enough to get the balloon out.
- Through that same hole you will poke pieces of the potpourri.
- Once the ornament is about half-full of potpourri, use the hot glue gun to glue the clipped ends of yarn back together.

- Make a hanger out of a piece of yarn or some satin ribbon.

- Now, hang your potpourri ornament where its sweet smell will fill the room.

The Main Thing:

The potpourri smells nice. It's been scented with all kinds of spices to give it that pleasant fragrance. The women went to the tomb to place spices on Jesus' body, which was the tradition of the day, but Jesus wasn't there.

Scented Play Dough

Resources Needed:

- Cinnamon
- Cream of tartar
- Flour
- Measuring spoon and cups
- Salt
- Saucepan
- Vegetable oil
- Water
- Waxed paper
- Wooden spatula

Resource Preparations:

Make Cinnamon Play Dough using the recipe below.

Recipe for Cinnamon Play Dough

- ¾ c. salt
- 1 ½ c. flour
- 3 T vegetable oil
- 1 ½ t cream of tartar
- 1 ½ c. water
- 2 T cinnamon

The cinnamon will naturally color the play dough a reddish-brown.

The Main Thing:

Name some spices that you have in your kitchen cabinets. Why do we use spices? In Bible times, they used many of these same spices to put on a body for burial. They didn't have funeral directors who embalmed the body, so they would put both liquid and powder spices on them. What does your mom or dad put your spices on?

When Jesus breathed His last breath, it was almost time for the Sabbath to begin. Jews did no work on the Sabbath and treating Jesus' body with the spices would have been considered work. So, they hurriedly placed Him in the tomb. Mary and the other women went there on the third day, hoping that someone would move the stone aside so they could go in and put the spices on Jesus' body.

What is one of your favorite spices? One that everybody uses and is probably the most popular is cinnamon. Cinnamon was also used in Bible times. We're going to use some play dough that has been scented with cinnamon. Oh my, it smells so good!

The Fun Stuff:

- Give the children a piece of waxed paper as a work surface.
- The children will use the play dough to recreate the scene in the garden with the stone over the opening to the tomb and the soldiers standing guard.
- They can work in small groups or individually to make the different parts of the scene.
- This is a wonderful exercise that will reveal what the children picture in their minds.

The Resurrection

Matthew 28:1-15

Read the Scripture passage in whatever version you prefer. We have chosen NIV (New International Version), which we find more kid-friendly.

Bible Story

After the Sabbath, at dawn on the first day of the week, Mary Magdalene and the other Mary went to look at the tomb.

There was a violent earthquake, for an angel of the Lord came down from heaven and, going to the tomb, rolled back the stone and sat on it. His appearance was like lightning, and his clothes were white as snow. The guards were so afraid of him that they shook and became like dead men.

The angel said to the women, "Do not be afraid, for I know that you are looking for Jesus, who was crucified. He is not here; he has risen, just as he said. Come and see the place where he lay. Then go quickly and tell his disciples: 'He has risen from the dead and is going ahead of you into Galilee. There you will see him.' Now I have told you."

So the women hurried away from the tomb, afraid yet filled with joy, and ran to tell his disciples. Suddenly Jesus met them. "Greetings," he said. They came to him, clasped his feet and worshiped him. Then Jesus said to them, "Do not be afraid. Go and tell my brothers to go to Galilee; there they will see me."

While the women were on their way, some of the guards went into the city and reported to the chief priests everything that had happened. When the chief priests had met with the elders and devised a plan, they gave the soldiers a large sum of money, telling them, "You are to say, 'His disciples came during the night and stole him away while we were asleep.' If this report gets to the governor, we will satisfy him and keep you out of trouble." So the soldiers took the money and did as they were instructed. And this story has been widely circulated among the Jews to this very day.

Key Elements:

Many people were crucified on crosses in that day, but none of them came back to life. None of them defeated death. No other religious leader in any religion has ever done what Jesus did by rising from the grave. This is a prime opportunity for children to understand that what Jesus did, dying on the cross and rising on the third day, was out of His love for each person. Children need to be given time to ask forgiveness and accept for themselves what Jesus did on their behalf.

Crushed or Not Crushed

Resources Needed:

- 4 uncooked eggs
- Egg carton
- Heavy book (at least 2 pounds)

The Fun Stuff:

- Place the eggs, pointy end down, in the egg carton and inform the kids that these are uncooked eggs, NOT boiled ones.
- Two eggs should be side-by-side one space in from the end of the carton, and the other two eggs should be side-by-side one space in from the other end of the carton. (A general rule is that the distance between the eggs should be about an inch less than the length of the book that you are using.)
- Let some of the kids experience the weight of the book.
- **Ask:** What do you think will happen if I put this book on top of these eggs? (Now, gently place the book on top of the eggs.) Did the eggs break? I sure thought those eggs would've been squished by that big book. But, they weren't. Amazing!

The Main Thing:

What is so amazing about Easter? Jesus did not stay dead. He was not "crushed" by Satan! We were surprised when the eggs weren't ruined, and, Satan must have been flabbergasted when his plan to crush Jesus in death backfired.

Mary in the Garden

Resources Needed:

- Artificial flowers and greenery
- Costume
- Fake rock

Resource Preparations:

- This is a first-person script for the telling of the Resurrection story and is a powerful way to present the events of those few days.
- It's told from Mary's point of view as she has returned to the garden to remember how her life was changed there.
- The Mary character should wear biblical attire and be seated in a garden you have created.
- One of the large fake rocks makes a good bench to sit on and then scatter lots of artificial flowers and greenery around her.

Mary's Script:

- (Mary enters) "Oh, it's just as beautiful as I remember it." (She sits and takes in everything around her.) "Would you mind if I shared with you what happened in this garden? (children respond) Please forgive me; I didn't introduce myself. My name is Mary, Mary Magdalene. My life was so messed up when I met Jesus, but He offered me the most wonderful gift—forgiveness. He forgave me and showed me how to live a life that pleases God. I feel rescued."

- "Not everyone wanted to accept His gift, and those very people had Him hung on a cross. When they took His broken body down from the cross, a man named Joseph of Arimathea offered to bury Jesus in his own grave…right over there. The Sabbath was beginning so Joseph buried Jesus quickly. I planned to come back as soon as the Sabbath was over, to put the burial spices on Jesus' body."

- "In the very early hours of the morning after the Sabbath, I headed out to this garden, carrying spices and perfumes for His body. Then, it dawned on me. That huge stone that the soldiers had rolled in front of the entrance of the tomb…how would I ever get it moved?"

- "I was terribly surprised when I got here, because that big stone had already been rolled aside. The tomb was open! I immediately started crying. I was sure someone had stolen Jesus' body. I stooped down and looked in the tomb. The cloths that had been wrapped around Jesus' body were folded there on the bench. And, two angels in the most gorgeous robes, dazzling bright, appeared there, one sitting at the head of the bench and the other at the foot."

- "Then, these men…these angels…spoke to me. They asked me why I was crying. Through the tears and sobs I cried, 'Because they've taken my Lord and I don't know where they've put him!' I had to get out of there, so I ran out. Someone was standing there, and I thought it was the caretaker of the garden. He also wanted to know why I was crying. So, I begged the man to tell me if he knew where they had taken the body of my Lord. Then, I heard my name, 'Mary.' It was the voice of Jesus saying my name. I wasn't talking to the gardener; it was Jesus standing there! He was alive! He was alive! Of course, I couldn't wait to tell the disciples. I ran as fast as I could to tell them that Jesus was alive."

- "That was the happiest moment of my life and it happened right here in this garden. Thank you for letting me share it with you."

Match Up

Resource Needed:

- 2 copies of the picture cards on card stock

Resource Preparations:

- Run 2 copies of the picture cards on Appendix 10.
- Cut them apart and then shuffle the cards.
- A child can play this by himself or several kids can play together.

The Fun Stuff:

- Place the cards face-down, individually in rows.
- Take turns drawing 2 cards.
- If the cards match, the player tells what the picture reminds him of from the last week of Jesus' life. Then he can keep the cards.
- The next person now chooses 2 cards. If the cards do not match, the cards should go back in the same position they were when chosen.
- The children will keep taking turns until all cards are picked up.

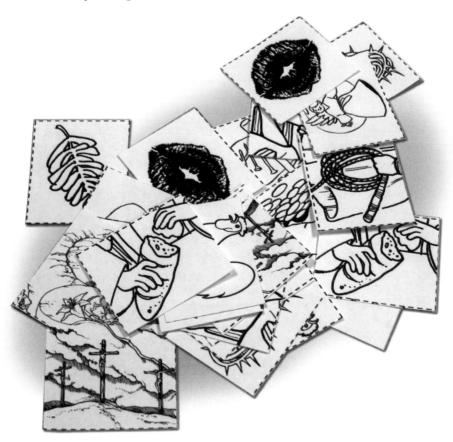

Altar Table

Resources Needed:

- Clay jars
- Crown of thorns
- Large candle
- Piece of muslin cloth
- Round concrete patio block
- Vase of flowers

Resource Preparations:

- Arrange all these things on a table where the children can see each object. (This would also be a very nice altar table for Easter Sunday in adult worship.)
- Go through each item and explain what it represents. You will have reasons you put it there (listed below), but let the children contribute what each item means to them also.

The Main Thing: (A list of symbols and their meaning for us)

Crown of thorns: (A real crown of thorns can be purchased online from www.holylandshopping.com for approximately $16 plus S&H.) They mocked Jesus and called Him the King of the Jews, and even put a sign at the cross that said it. Because they called Him a king, they made Him a crown, but it was out of a thorn bush. The thorns were long and sharp and dug into His scalp. (If you don't have a crown of thorns, you could use a rough cross instead.)

Clay jars: Because the Sabbath was beginning, Jesus' body was hurriedly placed in the tomb without being properly prepared for burial. After the Sabbath was over, some women came to the tomb with spices. They wanted to complete their tradition of putting these spices on the dead body.

Round patio block: When Jesus was placed in the borrowed tomb, a large stone was rolled across the entrance to ensure that none of His followers would steal the body and claim that He had risen. The women came to the tomb early in the morning and found the stone rolled aside.

Piece of muslin cloth: What the women found in the tomb was the shroud—the piece of cloth that had wrapped Jesus' body. It was in the place where He had been laid, but He was not there.

Vase of flowers: It was in the garden where Jesus had been buried that Mary Magdalene sat, mourning because Jesus was gone and she didn't know where He had been taken. Here in the garden she saw the risen Jesus and recognized Him when He said her name, "Mary."

Large candle: This light reminds us that Jesus is the Light of the World. When He conquered death, He conquered darkness. The lit candle chases the darkness out of a room. When Jesus is invited into a life, sin must leave so the Light can live there.

OBJECT LESSON

Toothpaste Surprise

Resources Needed:

- Long, skinny candy bar
- Toothpaste box

Resource Preparations:

- Before class, put the long, skinny candy bar in the toothpaste box and seal it so that it looks like it has never been opened.
- Choose one of the children to open the box.
- Everyone will be watching closely to see what is inside.

The Fun Stuff:

- Wait a minute! This isn't toothpaste.
- Now, if we had been expecting toothpaste and we needed to brush our teeth, this would have been a disappointment at first. This isn't going to work.
- I've really got to brush my teeth! My mom is going to be ticked if she sees that I have a candy bar instead of toothpaste.
- But then, when you think about the candy bar, you start thinking it's not so bad.

Why were you surprised when you opened the box? (It wasn't what you were expecting.)

The Main Thing:

When the women went to the tomb where Jesus had been placed after His death and found it empty, they were surprised. That's not what they were expecting to find there. When Peter and John came to the tomb and saw that Jesus was not there, they were surprised. It wasn't what they expected at all!

But the good news is this. They were sad because it wasn't what they expected, but it really was much better news. Jesus had risen from the grave! He was no longer there. He was alive!

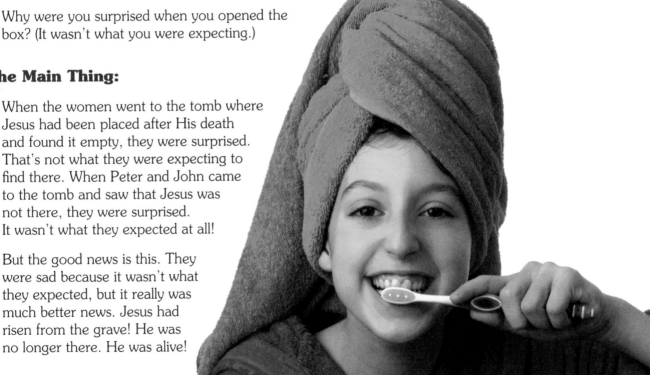

Trick Candle

Resources Needed:

- Cupcake
- Match
- Trick candle

The Main Thing:

- Place the candle in the cupcake. Make a big deal out of lighting the candle and draw attention to what you are doing.

- The Bible calls Jesus the Light of the World. But men killed Him and then buried Him.

- Blow out the candle. Did He stay dead? No, He rose from the dead.

- Watch the candle, because it will re-light.

- People thought they had gotten rid of Jesus, just as you thought I had blown out the candle. But God had other plans. God brought Jesus back to life and beat the hold that death had on Him.

- If we believe in Jesus as our Savior, the same thing will happen for us. Our bodies may die, but our souls will keep on shining in heaven with Jesus.

Road to Emmaus

Luke 24:13-35

*Read the Scripture passage in whatever version you prefer. We have chosen NIV
(New International Version), which we find more kid-friendly.*

Bible Story

Now that same day two of them were going to a village called Emmaus, about seven miles from Jerusalem. They were talking with each other about everything that had happened. As they talked and discussed these things with each other, Jesus himself came up and walked along with them; but they were kept from recognizing him.

He asked them, "What are you discussing together as you walk along?"

They stood still, their faces downcast. One of them, named Cleopas, asked him, "Are you only a visitor to Jerusalem and do not know the things that have happened there in these days?"

"What things?" he asked.

"About Jesus of Nazareth," they replied. "He was a prophet, powerful in word and deed before God and all the people. The chief priests and our rulers handed him over to be sentenced to death, and they crucified him; but we had hoped that he was the one who was going to redeem Israel. And what is more, it is the third day since all this took place. In addition, some of our women amazed us. They went to the tomb early this morning but didn't find his body. They came and told us that they had seen a vision of angels, who said he was alive. Then some of our companions went to the tomb and found it just as the women had said, but him they did not see."

He said to them, "How foolish you are, and how slow of heart to believe all that the prophets have spoken! Did not the Christ have to suffer these things and then enter his glory?" And beginning with Moses and all the Prophets, he explained to them what was said in all the Scriptures concerning himself.

As they approached the village to which they were going, Jesus acted as if he were going farther. But they urged him strongly, "Stay with us, for it is nearly evening; the day is almost over." So he went in to stay with them.

When he was at the table with them, he took bread, gave thanks, broke it and began to give it to them. Then their eyes were opened and they recognized him, and he disappeared from their sight. They asked each other, "Were not our hearts burning within us while he talked with us on the road and opened the Scriptures to us?"

They got up and returned at once to Jerusalem. There they found the Eleven and those with them, assembled together and saying, "It is true! The Lord has risen and has appeared to Simon." Then the two told what had happened on the way, and how Jesus was recognized by them when he broke the bread.

Key Elements:

Overcome with grief, the two men plod their way to a town seven miles away, Emmaus. Even though the men didn't recognize Him, Jesus walked alongside them, pointing out how scripture had foretold everything that had taken place. The children will learn how Jesus revealed Himself to these two men.

Balloon Sweep

Resources Needed:

- 7 pieces of construction paper
- Brooms
- Marker
- Water balloons (no water)

Resource Preparations:

- This game is best played in a very large open space (gym).
- Number seven pieces of construction paper from 1-7.
- Place these numbered cards in order throughout the space.
- Blow up a water balloon and tie it off for each team (no water, just air).

The Main Thing:

The Bible tells us that after Jesus had died and resurrected, two men who were walking to Emmaus were joined by a third man. The man asked them what they were talking about. Hadn't he heard what had happened to Jesus? Was he the only person who didn't know? The two men were kept from seeing that it was Jesus Himself walking with them. They walked together the seven miles to the town of Emmaus. When they reached Emmaus, the men asked Jesus (even though they didn't know it was Him) to come stay overnight with them. When Jesus broke the bread at dinner, all of a sudden the men realized who He was. Immediately, they ran all the way back to Jerusalem to tell the disciples they had seen the risen Lord!

The Fun Stuff:

- Each one of these signs represents a mile marker on the road to Emmaus. The starting point is Jerusalem.
- Station a player at each mile marker.
- The leader will place a balloon at the start line for each team.
- At the signal, the first player will use a broom to sweep the balloon to the first mile marker. When he arrives at mile one with the balloon, he will hand the broom to the person there, who will sweep the balloon on to the second mile marker.
- The broom will pass to the person at the third mile marker who will sweep the broom to mile four, and so on.
- When the balloon reaches the seven mile marker (or Emmaus), the team will shout, "It's the risen Lord!" and that person will have to sweep the balloon all the way back to Jerusalem (or the starting point).

Now We See Him

Resources Needed:

- Ammonia
- Cotton balls
- Goldenrod paper
- Small dishes
- White taper candle

Resource Preparations:

- Make sure you get real goldenrod paper and not just bright yellow paper.

- Beforehand, write "JESUS" on the goldenrod paper using the white candle.

- Go over the letters several times and then brush away any excess wax.

- You shouldn't be able to easily see that there is anything written on the paper.

The Fun Stuff:

- Dip the cotton ball in some ammonia and squeeze out the excess.
- Wipe the cotton ball across the paper from side to side, working your way down the paper.
- The paper will turn a reddish color and JESUS will appear.

The Main Thing:

When did the two men realize that it was Jesus who had accompanied them from Jerusalem? Even though Jesus talked with them and explained the scriptures as they walked, His identity was hidden from them, just like we couldn't see the word JESUS on our paper. But when Jesus picked up the bread and broke it at the meal, all of a sudden they realized who He was. They knew it was Jesus! He was revealed to them, just like the name JESUS was revealed to us on our paper.

More Fun Stuff:

- Dip a different cotton ball in some vinegar and squeeze out the excess.

- **Say:** When the two men realized who Jesus was, the Bible tells us that "at that moment he disappeared!" Jesus was gone!

- Wipe across the paper again using the vinegar cotton ball. This time the paper will return to its original color and you will no longer be able to see the letters written there.

Questions to be asked:

- How do you think the two men felt when they realized it was Jesus they were walking with?

- What did you think when JESUS appeared on the paper?

- How do you think the men felt when Jesus disappeared as quickly as He had appeared?

You've Been Recognized

Resource Needed:

- Ball cap

Resource Preparations:

- You'll need a space where all the kids can be standing. It's okay for other things to be in the room, but the group needs to be standing and spread out.

- In this game two players will keep their chins touching their chests so that their heads are down. It works best if these two players are some of the shorter kids in your group.

- Those two will turn their backs to all the other kids for just a moment while the leader places a ball cap on another child's head.

The Fun Stuff:

- At the signal, the two players will turn around and start their hunt to find the person who has the hat on. Remember, they cannot lift their chin from their chest.

- When they approach one of the kids in the group, they will have to try to feel their head to see if the hat is there since they won't be able to look up far enough to see if it's there.

- When the hat is finally found, the player will yell, "You've been recognized!"

The Main Thing:

Two men who had been followers of Jesus left Jerusalem and headed to Emmaus the day the women found the tomb empty. As they walked, they probably hung their heads because they were sad. Jesus was gone! While they were walking, another man joined them and talked with them all the way to Emmaus.

It was Jesus, but they didn't recognize Him. God caused them not to know who He was. It wasn't until Jesus broke the bread at dinner that they knew it was Him. That's when they recognized Him!

Jesus Appears to the Disciples

John 20:19-31

Read the Scripture passage in whatever version you prefer. We have chosen NIV (New International Version), which we find more kid-friendly.

Bible Story

On the evening of that first day of the week, when the disciples were together, with the doors locked for fear of the Jewish leaders, Jesus came and stood among them and said, "Peace be with you!" After he said this, he showed them his hands and side. The disciples were overjoyed when they saw the Lord.

Again Jesus said, "Peace be with you! As the Father has sent me, I am sending you." And with that he breathed on them and said, "Receive the Holy Spirit. If you forgive anyone's sins, their sins are forgiven; if you do not forgive them, they are not forgiven."

Now Thomas (also known as Didymus), one of the Twelve, was not with the disciples when Jesus came. So the other disciples told him, "We have seen the Lord!"

But he said to them, "Unless I see the nail marks in his hands and put my finger where the nails were, and put my hand into his side, I will not believe."

A week later his disciples were in the house again, and Thomas was with them. Though the doors were locked, Jesus came and stood among them and said, "Peace be with you!"

Then he said to Thomas, "Put your finger here; see my hands. Reach out your hand and put it into my side. Stop doubting and believe."

Thomas said to him, "My Lord and my God!"

Then Jesus told him, "Because you have seen me, you have believed; blessed are those who have not seen and yet have believed."

Jesus performed many other signs in the presence of his disciples, which are not recorded in this book.

But these are written that you may believe that Jesus is the Messiah, the Son of God, and that by believing you may have life in his name.

Key Element:

Jesus' resurrection is so unbelievable that Thomas refuses to accept what the disciples are telling him—that Jesus appeared to them. He wanted to see and feel the wounds on Jesus' body before he would be convinced of the disciples' story. Even today, we so often need to see God working in an obvious way before we'll believe that He really is present in our lives. The children will relate to Thomas' doubt.

Hanging Ice Cube

Resources Needed:

- A glass of water
- An ice cube
- Piece of string
- Salt

The Fun Stuff:

Say:

- I'm going to pick up this ice cube and take it out of the glass without using my hands. Do you believe I can do that?

- Submerge the ice cube in the glass of water for 2 seconds and then let it float on top of the water.

- Then, place one end of the string on top of the ice cube and sprinkle salt on the string and ice cube. Slowly, count to 5.

- Now, pick up the loose end of the string. The ice cube will lift right out of the glass and be hanging on the end of the string.

The Main Thing:

Let's talk about it:

You really didn't think I could get that ice cube out of the glass without using my hands. What made you believe it? You saw it actually happen. Jesus had told the disciples long before His arrest that He would die, but then He would rise again. That didn't sound real to them. It didn't sound possible. It wasn't until He appeared to them, and they saw Him alive again that they believed. Once they saw, they believed!

Some of the disciples had seen Jesus, but when they told Thomas, he wouldn't believe it was true. He said that he wouldn't believe until he could touch the wound in Jesus' side and the nail print in His hand. Jesus knew Thomas was having a difficult time believing in His resurrection. When Jesus appeared to Thomas, Jesus insisted that Thomas touch Him. Thomas believed because he saw with his own eyes.

Not There...and Now It Is!

Resources Needed:

- Cups of water
- Paint brush
- Plastic table covering
- White art paper
- White taper candle

The Fun Stuff:

- The kids will use a white taper candle to write the message "Jesus appeared" on a piece of white paper.

- This can be a challenge in itself, since it's difficult to see what you've written and where you are on the page.

- Once the message is completed, the children will paint their entire paper with watercolor paints.

- **Ask:** What happened when you put the watercolor paint on your paper? (The message suddenly appeared.)

- It was there all along, but it wasn't until we applied the paint that we were able to see the message.

The Main Thing:

Jesus mysteriously appeared to the disciples. One minute the disciples were just talking about what had happened to Jesus and the next minute there He was. They couldn't believe it was really Jesus, but Jesus showed them His hands and feet and then ate with them.

Breakfast with the Disciples

John 21:1-19

Read the Scripture passage in whatever version you prefer. We have chosen NIV (New International Version), which we find more kid-friendly.

Bible Story

Afterward Jesus appeared again to his disciples, by the Sea of Tiberias. It happened this way: Simon Peter, Thomas (called Didymus), Nathanael from Cana in Galilee, the sons of Zebedee, and two other disciples were together. "I'm going out to fish," Simon Peter told them, and they said, "We'll go with you." So they went out and got into the boat, but that night they caught nothing.

Early in the morning, Jesus stood on the shore, but the disciples did not realize that it was Jesus.

He called out to them, "Friends, haven't you any fish?"

"No," they answered.

He said, "Throw your net on the right side of the boat and you will find some." When they did, they were unable to haul the net in because of the large number of fish.

Then the disciple whom Jesus loved said to Peter, "It is the Lord!" As soon as Simon Peter heard him say, "It is the Lord," he wrapped his outer garment around him (for he had taken it off) and jumped into the water. The other disciples followed in the boat, towing the net full of fish, for they were not far from shore, about a hundred yards. When they landed, they saw a fire of burning coals there with fish on it, and some bread.

Jesus said to them, "Bring some of the fish you have just caught."

Simon Peter climbed aboard and dragged the net ashore. It was full of large fish, 153, but even with so many the net was not torn. Jesus said to them, "Come and have breakfast." None of the disciples dared ask him, "Who are you?" They knew it was the Lord. Jesus came, took the bread and gave it to them, and did the same with the fish. This was now the third time Jesus appeared to his disciples after he was raised from the dead.

When they had finished eating, Jesus said to Simon Peter, "Simon son of John, do you truly love me more than these?"

"Yes, Lord," he said, "you know that I love you."

Jesus said, "Feed my lambs."

Again Jesus said, "Simon son of John, do you truly love me?"

He answered, "Yes, Lord, you know that I love you."

Jesus said, "Take care of my sheep."

The third time he said to him, "Simon son of John, do you love me?"

Peter was hurt because Jesus asked him the third time, "Do you love me?" He said, "Lord, you know all things; you know that I love you."

Jesus said, "Feed my sheep. I tell you the truth, when you were younger you dressed yourself and went where you wanted; but when you are old you will stretch out your hands, and someone else will dress you and lead you where you do not want to go." Jesus said this to indicate the kind of death by which Peter would glorify God. Then he said to him, "Follow me!"

Key Element:

It was like the old days—Jesus telling the disciples (who were fishermen by trade) where to catch fish. I bet it was quite a breakfast as they all gathered around a campfire and roasted fish! Just as the disciples must have enjoyed being in Jesus' presence this one last time, in such a familiar setting, the children will enjoy putting themselves in the place of these devoted followers.

Ping-Pong Fish

Resources Needed:

- 153 ping-pong balls
- Butterfly nets
- Fish net
- Masking tape

The Fun Stuff:

- Recruit 2 or 3 people to hold the fish net open in one corner of the room.
- Pass out all the butterfly nets that you have and have them (catchers) position themselves in another part of the room. (Ideally, about one-third of your kids should have nets.)
- The rest of the kids (tossers) will have the ping-pong balls and should stand 10-15 feet away from the kids with the butterfly nets (catchers).
- Place a piece of masking tape on the floor as a line for the tossers not to cross, and another line 10-15 feet away that the catchers will have to stay behind when catching.

The Main Thing:

The Bible tells us that the disciples had not caught anything all night. Then, Jesus yelled to them to throw their net on the other side of the boat. When they did, the Bible says that they caught 153 large fish.

The Fun Stuff (continued):

- Today, our ping-pong balls are going to represent the fish and we're going to catch them in our butterfly nets.
- The tossers will bounce the ping-pong ball in the space between them and the catchers.
- Then, the catchers will have to snag the ping-pong ball in their net. Once three "fish" (ping-pong balls) are caught, the catcher has to run to the fish net that is being held in the corner and dump her catch there. As soon as the butterfly net is empty, she can return to her position to catch more fish. The tossers will be responsible for gathering up any stray "fish" (ping-pong balls) that weren't caught in the net so they can be re-tossed. The game is over when all 153 fish are in the net!

Breakfast Is Served

Resources Needed:

- 2 chairs
- 2 fish nets
- 2 inner tubes
- 2 plates
- 2 play campfires
- 2 skillets
- 6 poster board fish

Resource Preparations:

- Set up two parallel stations for this activity.
  Place each of the three stations at least 12-feet apart,
  further if you have the space for the kids to run.
- Station #1: Place a fish net on the floor and a chair about 4-feet away.
- Station #2: Place an inner tube on the floor.
- Station #3: Create a make-believe campfire. Put 3 poster board fish in a skillet and set a plate by the campfire.

The Fun Stuff:

- Divide the kids into two teams. (If you want to set up for more kids, just add more identical stations.)
- One player from each team will run the course.
- At Station #1, he will pick up the fish net and toss it over the chair. If it misses, he has to go pick it up and keep tossing until it goes over the chair.
- Then, he yells, "They didn't catch anything!"
- Then, he runs to Station #2. He will jump into the inner tube and pretend to be swimming while he says, "Peter swam to shore!"
- As soon as he's done that, he'll get up and run to Station #3 and sit on the floor by the campfire.
- The player will have to use the spatula to take the fish out of the skillet, one by one, and place them on the plate. As soon as all three fish are on the plate, he will yell, "Jesus made breakfast!"
- Reset the stations and the next two kids can go.

The Main Thing:

The kids will have a blast playing this sequencing game and be reviewing the story as they do. They'll never even know they've been in the middle of a learning experience.

Fish-y Pancakes

Resources Needed:

- Butter
- Fish cookie cutter
- Griddle
- Ingredients for pancakes
- Spatula
- Syrup

Recipe Ingredients:

- 1 c. flour
- ¼ c. barley flour
- 2 T sugar
- 2 T baking powder
- 4 T vegetable oil
- 1 egg
- Dash of salt
- 1 ¼ c. milk

*You can get fish sprinkles for the top of your pancakes from www.babykakes.com/sprinkles.

The Main Thing:

Jesus had a fire going and was preparing breakfast for the disciples when they reached the shore. Maybe He had the pan hot, just waiting for a couple of the fish they had caught. I don't know about you, but I don't normally eat fish for breakfast. But pancakes? Oh yeah! We'll just use a fish cookie cutter on our pancakes and pretend we're eating what Jesus fixed the disciples.

The Fun Stuff:

- Prepare the recipe for pancakes. (Or, if you'd rather use frozen pancakes, or ready-to-mix, it will work the same. I just love the homemade, though.)
- Mix the dry ingredients together before adding the wet ingredients.
- Ladle onto a hot griddle (350°).
- When the batter looses its shine, then flip to cook on the other side.

Use a fish cookie cutter to cut the pancake into a fish shape. Don't throw away the scraps, though. I'm sure someone will eat them, too.

Roll Over Those Fish

Resources Needed:

- Cardboard tray
- Construction paper
- Light brown craft paint
- Marble
- Paper plate

- Pattern for a fish
- Pencils
- Scissors
- Glue stick
- Transparent tape

The Fun Stuff:

- The children will use the fish pattern to draw more fish on different colors of construction paper. Then, cut them out and glue them to a 9" x 12" piece of construction paper.

- Use one piece of tape at each end of the construction paper to adhere it to the inside of a cardboard tray. (Canned goods come in these cardboard trays and you can gather them at the grocery store. Soda pop cans also come in these trays.)

- Squirt some brown craft paint on a paper plate and add a little water to it, so that it is fairly thin, but not watery.

- Roll the marble around in this paint and then lift it off the plate. Place it inside the cardboard tray and roll it around. When the paint has rolled off, re-dip it in the paint and roll some more. The marble will leave zigs and zags of brown paint all over the fish…and now you have a net.

- You can also create a net by preparing the paint in the same way, but use a flyswatter instead. Dab it gently over the top of the fish.

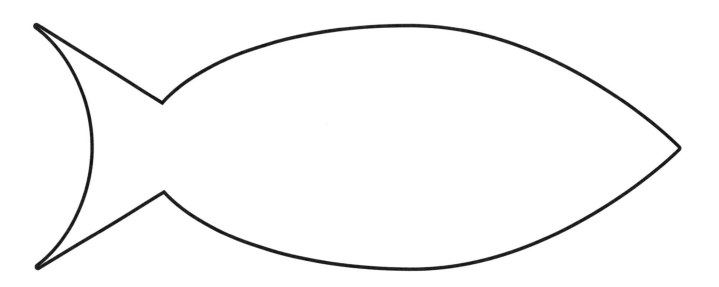

The Ascension and Great Commission

Acts 1:6-11

Read the Scripture passage in whatever version you prefer. We have chosen NIV (New International Version), which we find more kid-friendly.

Bible Story

So when they met together, they asked him, "Lord, are you at this time going to restore the kingdom to Israel?"

He said to them: "It is not for you to know the times or dates the Father has set by his own authority. But you will receive power when the Holy Spirit comes on you; and you will be my witnesses in Jerusalem, and in all Judea and Samaria, and to the ends of the earth."

After he said this, he was taken up before their very eyes, and a cloud hid him from their sight.

They were looking intently up into the sky as he was going, when suddenly two men dressed in white stood beside them. "Men of Galilee," they said, "why do you stand here looking into the sky? This same Jesus, who has been taken from you into heaven, will come back in the same way you have seen him go into heaven."

Key Element:

Jesus finally leaves this world and the disciples watch. With their mouths hanging open, they stare into the clouds until they can no longer see their Master. But, right before He disappeared, Jesus left them with His very last command; He told them to go make more disciples. He placed on them the mission to spread the news that everyone could receive salvation through believing in Jesus Christ. The children will be challenged by Jesus' last command, to go and do likewise.

Ascending Raisins

Resources Needed:

- Colorless soda (like Sprite or 7-Up)
- Fresh raisins
- Spoon
- Tall, clear glass

The Fun Stuff:

- Pour the can of soda into the glass. Then, drop 6 raisins into the glass.
- Do the raisins sink or float?
- Watch for a minute or two and see what happens.
- The raisins will rise in the glass. After a few seconds the raisins will go back down (and then will rise again and fall repeatedly.)
- We just want to observe through dropping them in, letting them rise to the top, and then letting them go back to the bottom.
- At that point, fish them out with a spoon.

The Main Thing:

Jesus came down to earth from His place in heaven. (*We dropped our raisins down into the soda pop.*) After completing His mission here on Earth—His birth, death for our sins, and resurrection—He gave His disciples their last instructions. It was now time for them to do what He had taught them to do. It was now time for them to spread the message of His coming.

Then, the Bible says that He disappeared into a cloud until they could no longer see Him. (*We don't know how it happened, but our raisins started coming to the top while we watched.*)

We call it ascension when Jesus went up into the clouds. Once Jesus was out of sight, angels came and talked with the disciples while they stood there with their heads thrown back, their mouths wide open, and watching…nothing.

The angels told the disciples that Jesus would return some day just like He left. (*The raisins were at the top and went back down to the bottom, which can remind us that Jesus will one day come back just as He said.*)

Stomp Rocket

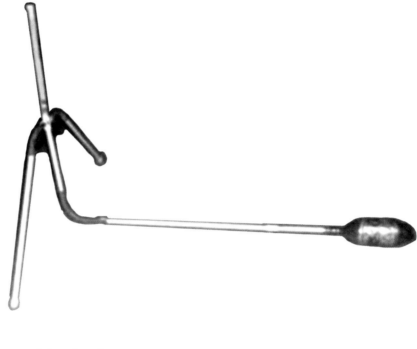

Resources Needed:

- Duct tape
- Empty 2-liter bottle
- File folder
- Plastic wrap
- PVC pipe

Resource Preparations:

- For complete instructions on how to make a stomp rocket, go to: www.sciencetoymaker. org/airRocket/index.html

- There are pictures on the website that will make it very easy to put together. It's basically made out of a file folder, PVC pipe, and an empty 2-liter bottle.

- We found that a file folder works better than the magazine pages they suggest for the rocket, though.

This stomp rocket is great fun when you can go outdoors. It will amaze you at how high it will go with a good stomp in the middle of the 2-liter bottle!

The Main Thing:

Ascension is a big word, but it's the word we use to describe what Jesus did when He left this earth. Ascend means to go up. The Bible tells us that Jesus was taken up in a cloud. He disappeared as the disciples stood looking up.

The Fun Stuff:

- Our stomp rocket ascended pretty fast. Do you think Jesus ascended that fast?
- How do you think He ascended?
- Our stomp rocket also returned to the earth. It came back just like it went up.
- The angels that spoke to the people who were watching Jesus ascend said that He would return in the same way that He left.

Toss Around the World

Resources Needed:

- Inflatable globes - Check Oriental Trading, www.orientaltrading.com for inflatable globes.
- Laundry baskets

Resource Preparations:

- The kids will repeat Acts 1:8, which says, "You will be my witnesses, telling people about me everywhere." Don't play the game until they feel like they can say this from memory.
- **SAY:** Jesus said to take His message to ALL of the world, so we're going to play a game with our inflatable globes.
- Set the laundry baskets against the wall.
- Then, determine a stand-behind line that will be an appropriate distance for tossing the globes.

The Fun Stuff:

- Designate a team for each laundry basket. At the signal, the first person on each team will toss the globe at the laundry basket.
- If it misses, then that person retrieves it and gives it to the next person on the team to try.
- When someone gets the globe to stay in the laundry basket, he says the verse very loudly… "You will be my witnesses, telling people about me everywhere."
- If you want to add questions about the story, you could discontinue play until the person who made the "basket" answers a question.

Questions for Fun Stuff:

- Who did Jesus want us to tell about Him?
- Where did Jesus tell us to go?
- What did Jesus tell the disciples to do?
- What happened when Jesus was done talking to the disciples?
- What did the disciples do when Jesus disappeared into heaven?
- What are we supposed to do today?
- Who do you know who needs to know about Jesus?

Appendices

Notes

Appendix 1
Angel Breakfast

Key Element:

- The Angel Breakfast is intended to be a special morning for grandparents and grandchildren, but could actually be any group that you determine.

- It can be used as an outreach program for inviting the neighborhood and community to "see" Easter in a new way, perhaps, and to get acquainted with your church.

- This is a brief outline of what could be included.

Menu

- Put little tent cards on each table with the menu posted.
- Sinless Sausage
- Crown of Jewels (Fruit Salad)
- Gabriel's Eggs-ellent Eggs
- Heavenly Hash Browns
- Jubilee Juice
- Golden Toast Sticks (French Toast)

Servers should be dressed in angel costumes. Halos can be made out of gold Christmas tinsel that is hot glued into a ring.

Decorations

- Set up round tables and cover with white cloth tablecloths. Put one ring of white lights (100 lights) covered by a thin white cloth on top of the table. Then, set gold spray-painted matte board castles on the top. Turn on all of the twinkling lights and turn off all the overhead lights.

- Place small, clear-plastic boxes of silver chocolate kisses tied with a white ribbon at each place setting. These will be the take-home favors. Use gold plastic dinnerware (fork and spoon) wrapped in a white napkin. Then, slide them through a gold wire angel napkin ring. Instruct your guests NOT to take the napkin rings, so you'll have them to use at another time.

- Make two posts from 4" x 4" x 8' lumber. Wrap them in white twinkling lights and add lightweight white material draped from the top to the floor.

- Add a bouquet of pearlized white balloons on top.

Photos

- Take photographs of each family standing with the Resurrection Angel.
- You can use one of the lit posts in the background. What a keepsake!

Resurrection Angel

- Find a man who will dress as the Resurrection Angel and present the monologue. (See Appendix 2 for Resurrection Angel Script.)
- A white tuxedo can be rented or purchased from a discount men's wear store. If you purchase one, try to make alterations without cutting any material off. Clear packing tape works great.
- Spray paint a man's tie with gold spray paint. Check a local theatre company for some feather wings and make a halo from gold Christmas tinsel.

Game

- Make an A-N-G-E-L Bingo game and play it with marshmallows.
- Give each person a small condiment cup with 20 mini-marshmallows in it to use as markers.
- The prize is an angel food cake, but be prepared for more than one winner.

Craft

- Make angels from a handkerchief-size piece of lightweight white material. (See Appendix 3 for Resurrection Angel Craft directions.)
- Put everything for the craft in Ziploc® bags along with directions.
- Set up separate tables in a different area for the craft.
- Encourage the adults to do the craft along with the kids.

Follow-Up

Send the pictures that were taken with the Resurrection Angel to the adults as a keepsake.

Appendix 2
Script for the Resurrection Angel

by Tina Houser

(Come out humming. The audience has gone unnoticed and then he stops abruptly to recognize them.)

Oh, hello. Maybe you can help me. I was invited to share breakfast with a group of people at _____. My GPS has been a little off lately since they sent that new satellite up. The old way sure seemed to work a lot better. By the smell of things, I must be getting close (kids will probably speak out). Oh, this is it? Well, hello again. Pastor _____ invited me to come so I could meet some of her very special little friends. Everyone who is a special friend of Pastor _____ say, "Hallelujah!" Oh, how I love to hear hallelujahs. How I love to sing hallelujahs (sing a line). How I love to surprise people and hear them yelp, "Hallelujah!"

Oh, by the way, I'm the Resurrection Angel. I was going to bring one of my fellow angels along with me, but he got another assignment, so I'm flyin' solo today. God has lots of special assignments for us. Sometimes we don't even realize what a big assignment we have. That's kind of what happened to my friend. God gave him an assignment about 2,000 years ago, in your time measurement. We were missing God's Son, Jesus, really badly in heaven. But, Jesus had an assignment of His own. God had sent Jesus to this earth to show people how to live, how to treat each other, how to love each other. It wasn't easy, but God sent Jesus anyway. The hardest part was knowing that Jesus came here to take the punishment for everyone's sins. Jesus was going to have to experience death to do that.

That's where my friend comes in. Jesus knew it was going to be difficult, so He went to the Garden of Gethsemane to pray. Jesus always talked everything over with His Father. As He bowed His head, God gave the immediate order that my friend needed to go and be by Jesus' side to give Him strength for the days that were coming. It was a good thing, too, because the guys Jesus had asked to pray with Him kept falling asleep. My angel friend brought strength straight from heaven to Jesus.

Now, I had an assignment of my own. I really didn't know what it was, but God had me working out at Jehovah's Gym. He said the assignment was going to call for me to be in shape (flex your angelic muscles). So, I was doing my repetitions and working with my coach.

There were some Jewish leaders down on earth that really didn't like Jesus. They got mad every time they heard Him talk about His Heavenly Father. One night, they sent soldiers to arrest Jesus. They beat Him with whips and sticks. They spit on Him and took His clothes. Then, they put nails through His hands and feet to hang Him on a cross. We all watched from heaven, waiting for God to do something. But, God was quiet. It was really strange. God watched His Son do the most difficult thing that has ever been done. God was in agony as He listened to the people make fun of Jesus. And then it was like someone turned on a loud speaker in heaven and we heard Jesus' words echo when He called out to His Father, "Forgive them, Father, they don't know what they're doing." As we looked at the ball that is Earth, it went dark. Jesus was dead.

All of heaven froze. We couldn't blink. What would happen now? God's Son was dead. We watched as Joseph of Arimethea took Jesus' body off the cross and placed it in his own tomb. Would we ever see Jesus again? Then, I heard God cry out for me. He meant business! I flew as fast as my wings would take me and bowed in front of God. He asked how my training was coming. I thought it was a strange question at such a sad time, but I told God I was as strong as a tow truck. "Good," He said, "because you're going to need it." Then, He whispered in my ear as I nodded my head. He turned to the rest of heaven and said, "You don't want to miss this. Get ready for a celebration." The angelic choir looked confused because they had just watched Jesus die. What was God celebrating?

Off I went to the tomb where they had buried Jesus. It had taken several soldiers to push a big stone in front of the opening, because they wanted to make sure no one stole Jesus' body. Then, God blasted on His miracle megaphone and said, "Move… that…rock!" (Extreme Home Makeover style.) I rolled up my sleeves, stretched a bit, and then gave a heave-ho and rolled that rock out of the way. I looked up and said, "Take Him away, God!" The angelic choir didn't even bother to warm up; they just burst into some mighty, high-powered hallelujahs!

But, my job wasn't done yet. I sat down inside the tomb to wait (whistling to pass the time). Sure enough, just like God told me, these women showed up to put spices on Jesus' dead body. Boy, were they surprised to see me! Of course, I did the old faithful "Fear Not" thing. I was the first one to tell His followers that Jesus was not dead. He wasn't there. He was alive again, just as He had told them He would be. Then, I said, "Shoo. Get out of here. Go tell His followers. They'll want to see this empty tomb for themselves." I sure didn't have to tell them twice!

We continued to watch Jesus surprise His followers over the next 40 days, showing up when they least expected it and proving that He was alive. Then He headed back to heaven. We're all busy now, getting heaven ready for all Jesus' believers to spend eternity with us in heaven.

Well, my assignment here is done. Got to get back to heaven…and I hope you'll be coming there some day too. I'll see you then.

Appendix 3
Directions for Resurrection Angel Craft

1. Cut out the wings from poster board. The pattern has already been drawn for you (*see* Appendix 4 for pattern).

2. Put 3 cotton balls in the center of the white square of material (or a handkerchief).

3. Pull the material around the cotton balls to make a head. Secure it by wrapping the gold chenille stick around the neck. Twist twice and leave the ends out (fairly equal in length).

4. Use a hole punch to make 2 holes where the dots are on the wings.

5. Outline the wings with a tiny stream of glue. Take the wings to the glitter station. Sprinkle glitter on the stream of glue and then shake it off over the pan.

6. Put a ring of glue around the head to make a halo. Take the angel to the glitter station and sprinkle with glitter. Shake off all the excess over the pan.

7. Attach the wings by pushing the ends of the chenille stick through the two holes. Twist the chenille sticks twice tightly against the wings.

You now have your very own resurrection angel to remember this special day.

Appendix 4

Angel Wings

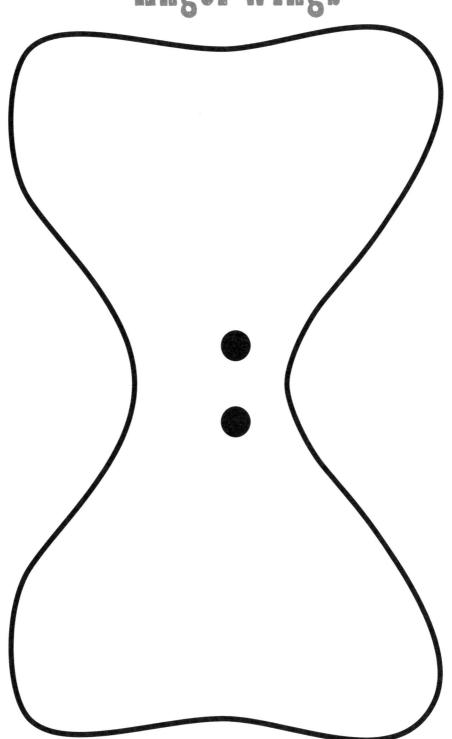

Appendix 5

Easter Egg Hunt for Special Needs Kids

Here's an outreach event that is very out of the ordinary. Put on an Easter Egg Hunt for kids who are normally disregarded when these events are being planned. Invite only kids who have special needs and challenges. That way, you can tailor it to their needs and give them plenty of opportunities for success.

Here's a report from a church that did this. Maybe this will get your juices flowing for a similar type event.

We got in touch with a teacher who works with these beautiful children and who was excited about our invitation. He works with 1st-5th graders and informed us that it could only be done during school time. I was hoping to get 70 dozen plastic eggs and enough candies to fill them, but when the church got wind of the plan, they supplied 3,000 filled eggs and prepared them for the kids.

We hid the eggs around our parking lot at the church so the kids could walk on the pavement and still reach into the grass to find their eggs. All of the eggs were hidden in plain sight so the children could find them easily. Because our church facility has islands in the middle of the parking lot, we had the perfect place to hide eggs for the kids in wheelchairs.

The school brought a helper for each of the kids. Some of them were teachers, teachers' aides, and even some kids from the elementary school who had earned the right to accompany the kids. It ended up that we had plenty of eggs for the kids who helped too.

The pastor gave a welcome and took a moment to tell the story of Jesus' death and resurrection. The entire event lasted about an hour and a half; then the kids got back on the busses and went to lunch at McDonald's. Before they left, though, we gave each of them a very pretty box with a chocolate cross in it. On the box was a sticker that gave our church name and the schedule for the Easter services.

The local paper came out to cover the egg hunt. The reporter said that in her eleven years at the paper, she had never heard of anything like this. Lives were touched that day, and it wasn't just the kids with special needs.

I don't know who had more fun—the kids or those of us who had the pleasure of filling the eggs, hiding them, and watching the smiles, hearing the giggles, and receiving the many hugs from these special kids. Those of us who were involved will always remember this day: "Inasmuch as ye have done it unto one of the least of these my brethren, ye have done it unto me (Matthew 25:40, KJV)."   —Cindy Coughlin

Appendix 6
Donkey Pattern

Appendix 7
Place Setting Pattern

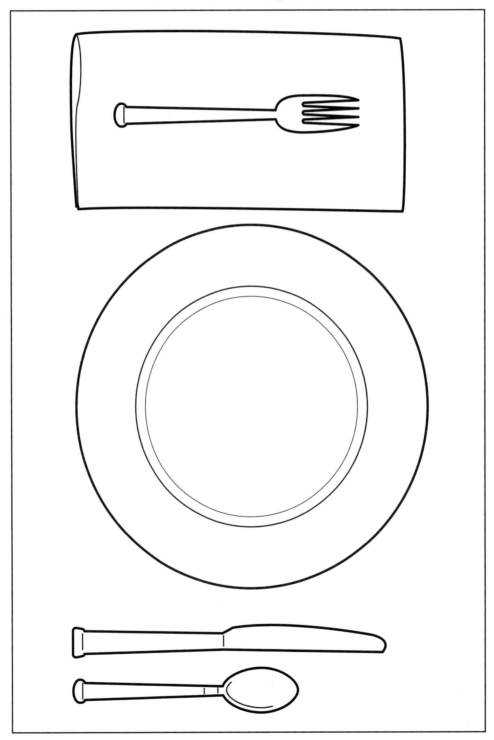

Appendix 8
Rooster Pattern

Appendix 9
Jelly Bean Dart Soldier

Appendix 10
Match Up

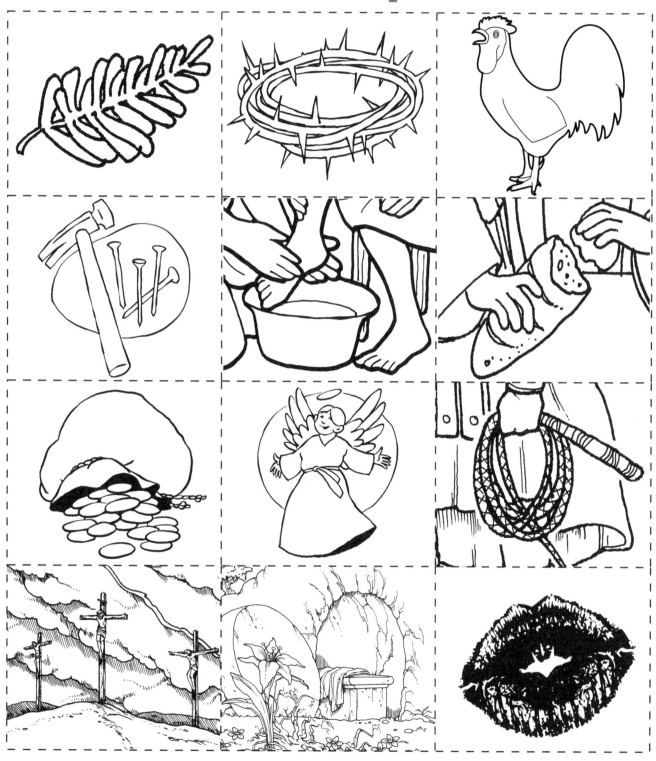

Notes